REINVENTING
THE SOVIET SELF

To Robert

REINVENTING THE SOVIET SELF

Media and Social Change in the Former Soviet Union

Jennifer Turpin

Westport, Connecticut
London

Library of Congress Cataloging-in-Publication Data

Turpin, Jennifer E.
    Reinventing the Soviet self : media and social change in the
former Soviet Union / Jennifer Turpin.
      p. cm.
    Includes bibliographical references (p.) and index.
    ISBN 0–275–95043–3 (alk. paper)
    1. Mass media—Soviet Union. 2. Soviet Union—Social
conditions—1970–1991. 3. Propaganda, Soviet—United States.
4. Soviet Union—Politics and government—1953–1985. 5. Soviet
Union—Politics and government—1985–1991. I. Title.
HN530.Z9M388   1995
306'.0973—dc20   94–22651

British Library Cataloguing in Publication Data is available.

Library of Congress Catalog Card Number: 94–22651
ISBN: 0–275–95043–3

First published in 1995

Praeger Publishers, 88 Post Road West, Westport, CT 06881
An imprint of Greenwood Publishing Group, Inc.

Printed in the United States of America

The paper used in this book complies with the
Permanent Paper Standard issued by the National
Information Standards Organization (Z39.48–1984).

10 9 8 7 6 5 4 3 2 1

Copyright Acknowledgments

The author and publisher gratefully acknowledge permission to reprint material from the following copyrighted source:

Excerpts from *Right in Her Soul* by Tracy B. Strong and Helene Keyssar. Copyright © 1984 by Tracy B. Strong and Helene Keyssar. Reprinted by permission of Random House, Inc.

Every reasonable effort has been made to trace the owners of copyright materials in this book, but in some instances this has proven impossible. The author and publisher will be glad to receive information leading to more complete acknowledgments in subsequent printings of the book and in the meantime extend their apologies for any omissions.

Contents

Illustrations

FIGURES

TABLE

Preface

This project developed out of my own personal experience of the Cold War. While traveling across the Soviet Union in 1986 to Nakhodka, to attend a conference on security and peace, I developed my interest in Soviet media. Everywhere the conference attendees went, booklets and newspapers were made available to us, all published by Novosti Press Agency. This was the material that so many dismissed as "propaganda;" after all, why were these English and other foreign–language publications available everywhere we went?

I collected as many of the materials as I could, and wondered if these forms of media didn't tell us something. If they were propaganda, wouldn't the materials tell us what sort of Soviet Union the officials wanted to convey? I began to wonder more; how are these materials put together, what is Novosti Press Agency in relation to TASS (Telegrafnoye Agentsvo Sovyetskovo Soyuza, Telegraph Agency of the Soviet Union), who are the actors and media principles operating behind these publications? How consistent is "propaganda," and what might any changes in its content tell us? How does the Soviet media handle foreign news compared to the United States? And why?

I began to study the Soviet press, and to read Novosti publications. I became especially intrigued with Novosti because as the U.S.S.R's foreign relations press, it was charged specifically with marketing the Soviet Union abroad. Most of the scholarship on Soviet media concentrated on domestic media, often with Cold Warrior Sovietologists (or Kremlinologists) decrying the public's indoctrination through news propaganda. In this research, I focus instead on media directed at the West in an attempt to understand which images were presented for American consumption and how they related to the social–political circumstances of the times.

Mikhail Gorbachev became general secretary (later president) just one year before my first travels in the Soviet Union; already his impact was felt and the term glasnost, or openness, had been introduced. Reading Gorbachev's speeches and statements to the press, I became fascinated with his blend of candor and politics grounded in a new interpretation of Leninism. His speeches were different from those of previous leaders; his pronouncements were sometimes shocking. Yet Gorbachev used the words of Lenin to legitimize his policies and declared his loyalty to the Communist Party. To analyze this more systematically, I decided to compare Novosti's publications under Leonid Brezhnev to those under Mikhail Gorbachev. As history unfolded, this project unveiled a process of change in the media, change in Soviet society, and change in international politics. Reading the history through the words of the Soviet media of events such as the Vietnam

War, Richard Nixon's visit to the U.S.S.R, Middle East relations, Soviet–China relations, the nationalist struggles in the developing world, and the Cold War, provided a great contrast with U.S. press coverage. Thus, I hoped to explore not only what happened to the Soviet press and how it affected the breakup of the Soviet Union, but also the function of the news media generally: when is propaganda news, and when is news propaganda? Can the process of generating "news" be democratic?

Many people influenced my thinking on these issues. Lester Kurtz encouraged me, often from great distances, over several years of my research. Gideon Sjoberg first introduced me to Soviet affairs—apart from the Cold War—which so many of us focused on. He also taught me a great deal about dilemmas in theory and methodology. To my good fortune, Thomas Cushman brought the first course on Soviet society to the University of Texas sociology department. Tom provided many insights about the troubled relationship between Sociology and Sovietology over time. He also gave me very useful feedback after he moved to Wellesley College. Sheldon Ekland-Olson provided me with a model of scholarship and teaching to try to emulate. I thank them all.

The discourse group and others at the University of California, San Diego encouraged me to pursue the problem of news and international relations. I am especially grateful to James M. Skelly, Hugh Mehan, Charles Nathanson, and Helene Keyssar. Thanks also to Tair and Timur Tairov for their support in the Soviet Union.

I thank Sanford Gottlieb for helping me get to the Soviet Union the first time. Dean Stanley Nel at the University of San Francisco has supported this research, as well as Associate Dean Gerardo Marín and the faculty development committee at USF, which provided me with two research grants. Adam Starkey provided valuable computer assistance. I also appreciate the support of James Ice, Liz Murphy, and Dina Rubin at Greenwood Publishing Group.

Finally, I thank my family and friends who have supported me over the years of this project, especially my mother Solveig Turpin. Most of all, I thank Robert Elias, for being my partner in love and life.

REINVENTING
THE SOVIET SELF

1

Introduction: Media Theory and Analysis

With the dramatic dissolution of the Soviet Union in recent years, many are speculating on the reasons for the collapse. Some have argued that the media played a central role; but little research has been conducted to examine the specific changes in media content and its impact under Gorbachev. This work begins to fill that gap. In conducting this research on the Soviet press, I used a discourse analytic perspective and applied sociological theory on impression management to the work of Soviet media organizations. Some argue that microsociological theory reveals little about institutions; I argue instead that it can help us understand how structural, as well as individual, impression management works. This theoretical approach led me to conduct an ethnographic content analysis, rather than only a quantitative analysis. This method of analysis makes more sense for answering the most important questions about the Soviet media.

DISCOURSE ANALYSIS

We can begin by understanding discourse analysis. "Discourse" has become a popular term in academic analyses, yet scholars seem to disagree about what the term means (Potter and Wetherell, 1987). Discourse analysis is practiced and developed simultaneously in fields as diverse as psychology, linguistics, sociology, philosophy, media and communication studies, literary studies, political science, and anthropology. The term has thus been used to refer to many kinds of research, from that concerned with language in its social and political context to structuralism and semiotics.

Here the term discourse analysis will be used in the more "macro" sense, referring to examining how language reflects its cultural origins and serves as a tool in constructing particular versions of social reality. A theme among discourse analysts emphasized here is that objective meaning does not said to exist; rather, discourses reflect multiple and often contradictory realities and shape the political relations in which they emerge, the institutions which provide their context, and the people who use them. In other words, no one discourse reflects the "truth" in any objective sense; rather, all discourses are selective. That selectivity is affected by and affects the individuals involved, the institutions in which discourse is based, and the political and social context. In essence, all discourse is political in that power relations are implicit in discourse; discourses are politically selective as they utilize certain concepts and frames while subjugating others. In attempting to ascribe meaning, alternative discourses are inevitably marginalized by the dominant discourse. All discourse, then, is rooted in power relations.

Dialogue is a primary condition of all discourse (Macdonnell, 1986); discourse analysis is based on the fact that all speech and writing is social. Discourses vary across and within countries, institutions, and situations (Volosinov, 1930, trans. 1973). According to Macdonnell:

> A "discourse," as a particular area of language use, may be identified by the institutions to which it relates and by the position from which it comes and which it marks out for the speaker. That position does not exist by itself, however. Indeed it may be understood as a standpoint taken up by the discourse through its relation to another, ultimately an opposing, discourse. (1986:2–3)

Discourse, then, becomes institutionalized, taking on a quasi–independent existence in opposition to other discourses.

This book uses this broader political conception of discourse, emphasizing the cultural and political nature of language. This research relies on a social psychological framework and attempts to better understand Soviet society by examining certain texts within their social context. Thus, it does not focus on discourse analyses concerned primarily with linguistic questions, work concerned with the relationship between cognition and discourse, individual ability to process texts, or semiotic research. Rather, it concentrates on research specifically examining the role of mass media in constructing various images and "definitions of the situation" that reflect who was in control of the Soviet press, the cultural assumptions about the role of the press, and the social and political context of the time.

DISCOURSE AND SOCIAL PSYCHOLOGY

Ethnomethodological research has developed this social–constructivist view of language, focusing on the notion that texts define reality and establish an interaction. Thus, texts are reflexive; they construct a certain reality that, in turn, has practical consequences (Garfinkel, 1967). In Harold Garfinkel's terms, the rules always embody an etcetera clause, in other words, meanings and rules of discourse are negotiated and altered with their context of use. Ethnomethodology, then, brings attention to the functional, constructive, and variable uses of language. Language is seen as a tool to create a particular social reality, or in Erving Goffman's (1959) framework, to manage impressions.

STRUCTURAL IMPRESSION MANAGEMENT

Anthony Giddens (1987) contends that Erving Goffman underestimates the relevance of his work for macrostructural sociology. While Goffman deals primarily with face–to–face interaction on the micro level, he states in *The Presentation of Self in Everyday Life* that the dramaturgical perspective, a view of social life as theater, has important implications at the structural level as well, that: "Any social establishment can be studied profitably from the point of view of impression management" (1959:238). This point of view suggests that human actors, and institutions, are geared toward managing impressions among selected audiences. Goffman's dramaturgical perspective describes the context in which discourse is constructed; the dramaturgical sphere of the theater provides a metaphor for institutions where discourse is manufactured.

Goffman introduces the notion of "teams," or persons (within an organization) who collaborate to create a particular definition of the situation. These teams are bonded by reciprocal dependency as they share information that could be detrimental to the performance and thus they depend on one another to remain loyal to the team. The goal of the performance team is to foster an impression and maintain it. The word team refers to members of any institution who are charged with maintaining the officially sanctioned image.

The audience constitutes another team interacting with the performer. Goffman emphasizes the importance of information control at the core of impression management. One of the ways of controlling information is to maintain two theatrical or organizational domains: a front stage and a back stage. The front stage is tidy, well kept, and entails politeness and decorum. This arena represents those aspects of organizations that are open to public scrutiny. The back stage, on the other hand, is more likely to be unkempt and informed, and allows for derogation of the audience. This theatrical sphere represents the hidden side of organizations. In general, audiences tactfully avoid the back stage, but often back stage control is difficult to contain. For Goffman, momentary lapses in back stage control are very important for the study of institutions, as they allow us to observe some normally hidden activity. In international relations, control of one's back stage is very important, as is trying to enter the adversary's back stage ("intelligence gathering") (Goffman, 1959).

INSTITUTIONS AS ACTORS

Can institutions and the manner in which they affect international relations through "what they say" via the printed word be treated as having human properties? Can organizations be treated as actors in global interactions? As Roderick Hart points out: "to conceive of how an institution 'speaks' is to risk committing some variety of anthropomorphic sin" (1984:31). The tendency to personify institutions as actors suggests reductionism. Clearly institutions do not think, feel, or behave in the literal sense. However, it is through institutions that the limits of individual rationality and capacity to handle information are overcome and major decisions are made (Douglas, 1986).

A significant amount of attention has been devoted to the debate concerning micro and macro approaches to sociology, with a fairly recent movement toward synthesizing or reconciling the two (Alexander and Giesen, 1987:26). Perspectives range from that of Randall Collins, who emphasizes the micro processes as "the glue that hold[s] structures together" (1987:195), to that of Niklas Luhmann (1987), who developed a version of functionalism which completely omitted the individual and group act, using the "system" as the unit of analysis.

Holding the middle ground in this debate are a number of scholars attempting to find the interconnections between micro and macro theory. A major book on the problem, edited by Alexander et al. (1987), reviews the micro/macro problem. Although the problem has received extensive treatment, the issue of the relationship of the individual to the organization is far from resolved. Most relevant to this research is the symbolic–interactionist perspective applied to international relations.

Several scholars (cf., Mehan and Skelly, 1988; Nathanson, 1988; Hallin and Mancini, 1988; Zimmermann, 1988; Richardson, 1988) have emphasized the process of interaction, approaching the study of international relations through discourse analysis, as a "global conversation." In this view, public political discourse is proposed to be *in some important ways* similar to discourse that regularly occurs in face–to–face encounters

(Mehan and Skelly, 1988). The verbal or printed "performance" is organized in anticipation of a response to occur via further media coverage or political acts, such as treaties, laws, or policies (Mehan and Skelly, 1988). Political discourse is seen as interactive; it is rooted in previous experience and constantly oriented toward the response it will generate. Discourse does not merely passively reflect what is going on in the world: "The choice of certain ways of talking constitutes different versions of the world and influences actual practice and the ways in which people think" (Mehan and Skelly, 1988:9).

A number of other media researchers have used the metaphor of the media as actor (cf., Arno, 1984; Dordick, 1984; Tehranian, 1984; Mowlana, 1984). According to Majid Tehranian (1984), media theories have variously described the mass media's role as "selfless revolutionaries," "fearless truth seekers," "responsible agenda setters," "benign gatekeepers," "development promoters," "hidden persuaders," and "sinister manipulators." A useful metaphor used by several researchers is that of media as storyteller (cf., Tuchman, 1978; Arno, 1984). In other words, the media, as an institution, constructs stories that are embedded in particular social, historical, and political contexts. This metaphor captures both the cultural and the socially constructed nature of news. In addition, the media allows for variation in form that news takes in different social and historical contexts. Implicit in this research on Soviet news is the fact that the story may be more or less bound by political features of the culture in question and subject to organizational requisites.

Language constitutes a feature of society that individuals and institutions share. Giddens argues that one of the most obvious examples in Goffman's work of the recursive nature of the structural qualities of social systems is language. Giddens states: "The generalized procedures of language use, are not properties of any individual subject, but of language communities stretching across very long spans of time–space" (1987:135). Thus, to treat language as only a feature of the micro dimensions of social life ignores the saliency of discourse in the structural realm. However, neither the actor nor the organization can be eliminated from an analysis of the context and processes by which discourse is used.

THE "ADMINISTERED SOCIETY"

Some peculiar features of Soviet bureaucracy also affected the role of the media there. Historically the bureaucratism of Soviet society had important consequences for the press. Alexander Yakovlev, Gorbachev's close ally, claimed:

> Bureaucratism is a kind of legalized lawlessness. It is a
> condition in which common sense and the real interests of
> the individual and society are sacrificed to the unlimited
> power of bureaucrats and office routine. (Cohen and
> Vanden Heuvel, 1989:50)

Max Weber characterized bureaucracies as having formal written rules, a hierarchy of authority, a division of labor and specialization, a standardization of human action, and an emphasis on efficiency and rationality (1946). The Soviet press epitomized this model, but revealed additional patterns evident in bureaucratic organizations not addressed by Weber.

The problem of hidden arrangements has been raised as a central theoretical and moral problem of bureaucracies (Sjoberg, Vaughan, and Williams, 1984; Williams, Sjoberg, and Sjoberg, 1983). Institutionalized secrecy systems within the Soviet press have been justified by the prerogatives of Soviet mass communications. Consistent with prevailing ideological doctrine, definitions of truth, rationality, and efficiency historically reflect different cultural conceptions from those reflected in Western institutions, thereby leading to disclosure of information on a different basis of selectivity. "Truth," "rationality," and "efficiency," historically refered to that which advanced the cause of Marxism–Leninism, therefore, the ends were determined a priori. The means to achieve the given ends varied according to the directives of the current leadership. For example, under Stalin only one perspective was permitted to be conveyed by the press, while under Nikita Khrushchev, greater flexibility was seen as consistent with Khrushchev's interpretation of the agenda of socialism.

One notable cultural difference lies in the historical definition of efficiency; timeliness was never a priority of the Soviet press. Coverage also reflects different cultural priorities; often events that would have been covered in the Western press were not reported at all in the Soviet press (Mickiewicz, 1981). For example, murders and other violent events fill the pages of Western media, while these occurrences were not seen as pertinent to the advance of socialism and were therefore not attended to by the Soviet press. Thus, "secrecy" in terms of responsibility in press reporting reflects, in part, different cultural norms. However, the deliberate choice of party and government elites to prevent coverage of news that is vital to the public reflects their attempts to maintain power. For example, the Chernobyl disaster, while widely viewed as a watershed in terms of openness of the Soviet press and polity, was not reported to citizens for days. The aftermath of Chernobyl did help to provoke glasnost, as the Soviet government began to realize the difficulty of suppressing such news.

Maintenance of a system of secrecy relies on cooperation from subordinates who have access to important information (Sjoberg, Vaughan, and Williams, 1984), or as previously discussed, the performance team. The formidable training of Soviet journalists, the elaborate system of censorship, and an ideological doctrine fostering loyalty to the organizations that prevailed in the Soviet Union have historically served to maintain an official consensus regarding what is newsworthy. The coercive power maintained by organizations in the Soviet Union served to overshadow the individuals comprising them.

Not to be disregarded is the system of perks granted to those with party and government status that served to maintain the official consensus. The privileges received by the *nomenklatura*, combined with coercive threats, served as powerful incentives to maintain the official definition of reality. As those in powerful positions received greater benefits, the organizational bureaucracy also fostered stratification (Sjoberg, Vaughan, and Williams, 1984), which in turn facilitated organizational stability.

While individuals have been historically condemned, relegated to nonperson status, and rehabilitated in the Soviet Union, organizations were rarely called on to account for their actions, as they generally represented subsidiaries of the state. An inherent tension existed between the individual and the organization, with citizens relying on large bureaucratic institutions, yet at their ever present mercy.

Interlocking directorates or "incestuous" relations between elites in various government, party, and press organizations also contributed to an abuse of power fostered by organizations and their ruling elite. Managers of the press organizations were generally recruited from the Communist Party and government posts and often returned to those roles after some service.

The relationship of the organization to the market also differed in the Soviet Union from that of the West. In the United States, for example, what the press publishes is necessarily related to what "sells." In the U.S.S.R., historically, news was centrally planned, like so many aspects of cultural life; however, that relationship began to change under Gorbachev and more Western styles of news production and coverage are still emerging. Those changes can be documented by examining media frames over time.

MEDIA FRAMES

Erving Goffman's notion of "frame" provides a theoretical concept which bridges the social–psychological and organizational realms of storytelling; he contended that in order to negotiate and comprehend reality, we frame it. Goffman defines a frame as "the principles of organization which govern events—at least social ones—and our subjective involvement in them." Frames organize strips of everyday affairs; a strip defined as "an arbitrary slice or cut from the stream of ongoing activity" (Goffman, 1974:10–11). Goffman's work has been developed and extended to the organizational level in research on mass media (cf., Tuchman, 1978; Gitlin, 1980), in which the concept of media frames is used. Media frames organize the world for both the journalists who cover it and for the audiences who attend.

> Media frames are persistent patterns of cognition, interpretation, and presentation, of selection, emphasis, and exclusion, by which symbol–handlers routinely organize discourse, whether verbal or visual. (Gitlin, 1980:7)

For organizational reasons, media frames are unavoidable (Gitlin, 1980). They allow journalists to process information in a highly efficient manner and to package it for organized dispersal to their audiences. By utilizing media frames, producers of news construct a view of reality rather than simply report it (Tuchman, 1978). The social-psychological and organizational dynamics of media framing are tightly coupled, yet these processes often go unrecognized.

As a socially constructed reality, news gives phenomena their public character (Tuchman, 1978). In other words, news organizations determine which issues receive newsprint, and therefore, what is newsworthy. Newspapers impart to a giant population of dispersed ethnic groups the capacity to access selected cases of the occurrences in each other's lives. Additionally, news enables policy makers to send messages to one another: to make their programs known without discussing them directly. The news serves as a testing ground for the reactions of others in power.

According to Tuchman (1978), the public character of news suggests its role as a social institution. First, news is a social institution that avails certain information to news consumers. Second, news is an ally of legitimated institutions. Only certain personal figures have access to utilizing the news for their own or their organization's needs. The average Soviet citizen could not walk into a press office and influence the agenda, but certainly the political elites surrounding Gorbachev could. Third, news is located, gathered, and distributed by professionals who work for organizations. News, then, is a product resulting from substantial socialization of news professionals to accepted norms and from conforming to the formal and informal rules of their organizations.

The dramaturgical perspective designed for microlevel analysis may be extended to the level of the organization while emphasizing that the institution has features above and beyond those of its sum of individuals. In addition, the boundaries imposed on the media by the social structure and the organization must be addressed. Weber's "iron cage" metaphor, which attended to the idea that institutions take on lives of their own, independent of the individuals comprising them, clearly applies to mass media organizations. In the case of the Soviet press, the institution was historically organized to achieve certain goals defined by elites, particularly that of impression management (propaganda and agitation). Particular features of the organization may contradict its overall mission, such as incidents in which actors (or organizations) accidentally disclose back stage information and then try to remedy the image damage (as Goffman [1959] noted in his description of slips, embarrassment, and saving face). The concept of media frame attends to these social–psychological processes and to the structural demands of news construction.

Goffman's (1959) notion that teams maximize impressions suggests that a foreign relations press, such as Novosti Press Agency, would direct enormous energy toward impression management in the global arena. Novosti was designed explicitly for presenting information about the U.S.S.R. to the non–Soviet world, and information control has been a very important aspect of that mission, particularly within the historical context of the Cold War.

In the case of the Soviet press, impression management dominated earlier publishing agendas; alternative discourses were subverted by a complex system of social control. However, as will be demonstrated, new media frames emerged under Gorbachev's leadership.

METHODOLOGY

The research for this project included an ethnographic content analysis of Novosti publications from January 1988 to January 1990 during Gorbachev's leadership and January 1972 through January 1974 during Brezhnev's leadership, to determine continuities and changes in any aspect of media presentation. The content analysis was supplemented by information regarding the structure of Novosti and changes occurring in the Soviet mass media system, as well as in Soviet society more broadly.

Ethnographic content analysis can be defined as the reflexive analysis of documents (Plummer, 1983), and is utilized to document and comprehend the communication of meaning and to explore theoretical relationships (Altheide, 1987). An ethnographic content analysis requires the researcher to approach the subject matter reflexively and interactively with a systematic but not too rigid mode of data collection and analysis. The method of discovery is employed throughout all stages of the investigation, therefore the researcher, concepts, data collection, and the analysis are said to "interact" (Altheide, 1987).

Both qualitative and quantitative methodologies begin with "a long preliminary soak" in the materials (Hall, 1975:15). The issue then is whether to identify countable categories and investigate their recurrence, or to use "the preliminary reading to select representative examples which can be more intensively analyzed" (Hall, 1975:15). I chose to do both. I selected key areas of news for their political significance and compared the frames of the issues in two time periods. An ethnographic content analysis supplemented with some quantitative measures is proposed to be most fruitful, as the data on Soviet political culture cannot be easily separated into distinct categories; they are dialectically interrelated.

An outline of the differences between ethnographic content analysis (ECA) and quantitative content analysis (QCA) provided by David Altheide (1987) will clarify the research program employed in this project. The research goal in ECA is discovery as well as verification, while the goal in quantitative content analyses is generally verification. In addition, the research design is reflexive and emphasizes validity, often described as the accuracy of a measure, while QCA generally focuses on reliability, or the consistency of a measure. While QCA progresses from data collection to analysis and interpretation in a serial manner, ECA moves reflexively and circularly. The primary researcher, who has received substantial training prior to collecting the data, is actively involved in all stages of the research program in ECA, rather than only the data analysis and interpretation stages.

The method employed in ECA generally involves purposive and theoretical sampling, some prestructured categories, numerical and/or narrative data, and multiple data entry points. QCA, on the other hand, usually applies random or stratified sampling, all prestructured categories, solely numerical data, and one data entry point. Narrative description and comments are always included in ECA, including concepts that emerge during the research. The analysis may be both textual and statistical, and data presentation often includes tables and text.

The choice of the ethnographic vs. the quantitative method does not amount to a choice of the intuitive over the objective. Both methods rely on "preliminary interrogations of the material, interrogations which proceed, at least implicitly, from 'intuitive' assumptions about what matters in the content, what needs to be either analyzed or counted" (Gitlin, 1980:304). Stuart Hall argues that:

> The error is to assume that because content analysis uses precise criteria for coding evidence it is therefore objective in the literal sense of the term: and because literary/ linguistic analysis steers clear of code–building it is merely intuitive and unreliable. Literary/linguistic types of analysis also employ evidence: they point, in detail, to the text on

which an interpretation of latent meaning is based; they indicate more briefly the fuller supporting or contextual evidence which lies to hand; they take into account material which modifies or disproves the hypotheses which are emerging; and they should (they do not always) indicate in detail why one rather than another reading of the material seems to the analyst the most plausible way of understanding it. Content analysis assumes repetition—the pile–up of material under one of the categories—to be the most useful indicator of significance.

Literary/linguistic and stylistic analysis also employs recurrence as one critical dimension of significance, though these recurring patterns may not be expressed in quantifiable terms. These recurring patterns are taken as pointers to latent meanings from which inferences as to the source can be drawn. But the literary/linguistic analyst has another string to his bow: namely, strategies for noting and taking account of emphasis. Position, placing, treatment, tone, stylistic intensification, striking imagery, etc., are all ways of registering emphasis. The really significant item may not be the one which continually recurs, but the one which stands out as an exception from the general pattern—but which is also given, in its exceptional context, the greatest weight. (1975:15)

Quantitative content analysis can yield important information in media analysis, but in light of the issues examined herein, a qualitative analysis supplemented with quantitative measures is preferred. A quantitative analysis may tell us, for example, how many times the word Stalin occurs in newsprint, but will not tell us *how* Stalin is talked about. Additionally, the changing boundaries of acceptable news coverage in the Soviet Union often render the newly discussed, but not necessarily recurring issue or theme, of great significance.

Employing the methods of ECA supplemented with some QCA, the following three types of news features were explored as pre–structured categories:

1. News related to the Soviet Union's political relations with the external world, particularly east–west relations. The analysis especially focuses on features regarding U.S.–Soviet relations and military policy.
2. Stories related to the internal social, political, and economic sphere. In this category, I will emphasize Soviet social policy, economic arrangements,

"pluralism" in Soviet politics, and human rights issues, as these all have implications for the Soviet Union's image abroad and its relations with other nations.

3. Letters to the editor are compared in terms of the issues outlined in 1 and 2.

Data sources include the following Novosti publications directed toward the West, and printed in English:

a. *Moscow News*: published weekly in nine languages including Russian and English.

b. *Soviet Life* (U.S.): published monthly as part of an exchange agreement between the U.S. and Soviet governments.

This data is not argued to be "valid," in the sense that it is "accurate" or unbiased. Instead, the sources are used explicitly for the purpose of studying impression management at the macro level; therefore, they are said to be "valid" only in the sense that they reflect institutional attempts at managing impressions.

The time periods were selected for comparison on the basis of the theoretical relationship between political context and the mass media. The Brezhnev era was selected due to its conservative climate relative to the more recent Gorbachev period. The years 1972 to 1974 were selected because Brezhnev solidified his power just prior to that time by arranging key positions of leadership around him, and also because his power declined markedly before his death in 1982 (Hazan, 1987). The Gorbachev years were selected for recency.

In subsequent chapters I will overview the assumptions that guided the Soviet media system over time. I then examine the particular history of Novosti Press Agency, which was central to the Soviet media system as the foreign news service. The development of Novosti's two major publications directed toward the West—*Moscow News* and *Soviet Life* —are analyzed and the changes in media framing and content in these publications over the Brezhnev and Gorbachev periods are examined. I conclude by examining how changes in media structure and content influenced the course of events in the Soviet Union, and ultimately contributed its breakup.

2

Soviet Political Communication

In this book, I examine the role that mass media played in creating immense social change in the former Soviet Union. The image of the "old" Soviets, maintained under Brezhnev, is investigated and contrasted with the "new" Soviets constructed under Gorbachev. The process of "reinventing" the Soviet national image—a feat accomplished by Soviet mass media organizations—is examined with a focus on the most significant organization engaged in its reinvention: the (formerly Soviet) press agency Novosti. To understand the central role that media played in this process, I will begin by examining the historical role of mass media in the Soviet Union.

THE HISTORICAL ROLE OF MASS MEDIA IN THE SOVIET UNION

The notion of what constitutes a free versus an unfree press is rooted in each society's political and economic system and its culturally defined ethics. Thus, a U.S. definition of press freedom emphasizes the degree of government control or regulation, while a Soviet measure of press freedom stresses the degree of private control or ownership (Hopkins, 1970). The press must be viewed in light of the philosophical assumptions that prefigured the Soviet mass media system.

THE INDIVIDUAL AND SOCIETY

The Russian tradition, in striking contrast to American tradition, emphasizes the communal nature of human life rather than individuality.

This tradition was partly shaped by the Russian Orthodox Church. Separated from the Reformation and the Scientific Revolution, Russian political culture remained outside the Western movement toward individualism and autonomy. The church remained a dominant force for subordinating the individual to God's will, to the czar, and to the collective. These cultural imprints prefigured the ethic of *partinost*, or loyalty to the party (Cushman, 1991).

The Bolshevik Revolution, inspired by the belief that the masses could alter society through communal action, challenged this concept of human passivity, posing instead the possibility—among other things—of an active, independent, people's press. But Lenin, in his work "What is to be Done?" was obsessed with party organization, centralization, and ideological unity. He defined a different role for the Soviet mass media: it would be an instrument of mass persuasion and agitation (Fitzpatrick, 1984).

CENSORSHIP AND THE SOVIET JOURNALIST

Press control was quickly established after the revolution, consistent with Lenin's definition of the newspaper as collective propagandist, agitator, and organizer (Hollander, 1972). After Lenin's death, Stalin embraced Lenin's media philosophy, while Khrushchev used more conciliatory terms such as "Communist education" to describe the press' role (Hazan, 1976). During the post–Stalin era, the press system expanded voraciously. In 1957 a Union of Journalists was formed, and by November of 1959 more than 700 delegates attended its first All–Union Congress in Moscow. By the second conference in October 1966, membership had reached 43,000, making the Union of Journalists the largest professional union in the country (Hollander, 1972).

The journalist's role remained defined by loyalty to Marxist–Leninist theory, and publishable material had to meet the following criteria:
1. Party–mindedness or unconditional party loyalty (*Partinost*)
2. High ideological content (*Ideinost*)
3. Patriotism (*Otechestvennost*)
4. Truthfulness (to Leninist theory) (*Pravdinost*)
5. Having a popular character (*Narodnost*)
6. Accessibility to the masses (*Massovost*)
7. Criticism and self–criticism (*Kritika i Samo–kritika*)

A Soviet journalist's socialization focused on applying these criteria properly, and writers were regularly informed as to what, currently, was politically sanctioned writing (Hollander, 1972).

The redundancy of Soviet press control organizations shows the complexity of the problem of social control. The Russian system of book censorship has been in place since Czar Fedor II's reign (1676–1682). In 1922, the Soviet government reinstated the czarist censorship agency, calling it Glavlit—the Chief Administration for Literary and Publishing Affairs (Hopkins, 1970). The organization approved all printed matter before publication and monitored newspapers and publishing organizations. In 1953 the name was changed to the Chief Administration for the Protection of Military and State Secrets in the Press, and in 1966 the word "military" was dropped (Hopkins, 1970). The organization continued surveying Soviet mass media for political and ideological content, despite the system of self–censorship that had become ingrained in most Soviet journalists.

Besides Glavlit, several government agencies monitored Soviet mass media. The committee on the press, disbanded in the early 1930s, was reinstated under Khrushchev in August 1963 to oversee publishing in newspaper and magazine plants. During the first few years of the press committee's reinstatement, Glavlit operated under its direction, but was transferred to the Council of Ministers in 1966 (Hopkins, 1970).

The Department of Propaganda, usually supervised by a Politburo member, had ultimate authority over mass media coordination. It appointed people to editorial and management positions to oversee the operations of official and "unofficial" organizations such as Novosti (Hazan, 1976). A "revolving door" existed among party and government officials, the official press, and the "unofficial press agency" Novosti. The mass media's role and structure remained intact until changes were introduced by Gorbachev.

THE SOVIET PRESS UNDER GORBACHEV

> Broader publicity is a matter of principle to us. It is a political issue. When the subject of publicity comes up, calls are sometimes made for exercising greater caution when speaking about the shortcomings, omissions, and difficulties that are inevitable in any ongoing effort. There can only be one answer to this, a Leninist answer: Communists want the truth, always and under all circumstances. (Gorbachev, February 26, 1986)

In the early days of Gorbachev's leadership, the press was baffled by his unprecedented statements. His speeches were generally edited and published days after they were given. The Soviet press was said to be "unable to stomach the highly controversial issues raised by Gorbachev" (Hazan, 1987:165). As the Soviet specialist Thomas Remington put it: "Under

Gorbachev the orchestra has begun performing in a new key" (1988:28). After three or four months Gorbachev consolidated his power over the press. He appointed Alexander Yakovlev, former Ambassador to Canada, to the important post of chief of the CPSU (Communist Party of the Soviet Union) Central Committee Propaganda Department. Yakovlev also served as head of the Soviet Institute for World Economy and International Relations and was a close friend of Gorbachev (Remington, 1988). Previously, Yakovlev had been assigned to diplomatic exile in Canada since he was incompatible with Brezhnev's clan. Yakovlev is seen by many as the reform spokesman behind Gorbachev, and as the person who initiated the radically changed rhetoric about the conflict between East and West.

Gorbachev's three–part approach to change in the Soviet Union— perestroika, glasnost, and demokratizatsiya—received mixed reviews, mainly because Gorbachev's economic reforms had failed. Glasnost was applauded in Western reviews (e.g., Isaacson, 1989), and in Soviet polls (Marinov, 1989). Free expression in the Soviet Union blossomed at an unbelievable pace; the most astonishing consequence of this growth was the overturn of the Communist Party monopoly of Soviet politics.

Michael Urban has shown that Gorbachev's own speech patterns displayed more openness than the traditional Soviet leader's pattern, which he calls "the classic Leninist tale." Two elements of Gorbachev's language distinguished his discourse from Konstantin Chernenko's. The first change was that his language included uncertainty. At times, Gorbachev admitted that he did not have all the answers, and he avoided giving authoritative prescriptions for what needed to be done in the Soviet Union. Instead, Gorbachev spoke about the need to deeply analyze the nation's problems, and stressed the need to change social relations and practices instead of blaming individuals and the past for current problems (1988).

Gorbachev's language also acknowledged the public's desire to participate in change rather than merely view it as spectators. In these ways, the Soviet leader loosened the constraints imposed by the regime's official definition of the world, opening greater social space for communication. In Urban's semiotic terms, Soviet political language moved from "mythic" to "practical." This had an important impact on the possibilities for political change. In fact, new myths were being fashioned, but they appeared more practical myths. Thomas Remington (1988) noted Gorbachev's use of "theoretical key words," or semantics, that drew attention to his programs and differentiated them from those of his predecessors.

Historically, the Soviet Union exerted tremendous resistance to the Western press and Western styles of mass media presentation. Yet eventually Soviet elites actually appeared in many respects to have adopted Western styles of presentation (Skelly, 1989). The mass media traditionally took its direction from party and government propaganda departments. But as

Mickiewicz (1988) has suggested, this relationship weakened as a result of demands for multiple perspectives in the news.

While socialism historically guided the Soviet press, the Western press professed to accuracy and objectivity as ideal criteria for the news (Skelly, 1989). The Soviets moved toward the Western view of the media as an instrument for advancing "public opinion," including a shift in emphasis from the group to the individual (Mickiewicz, 1988), which was partly reflected in the rapid growth of advertising in Soviet newspapers and magazines.

The Soviet press historically served as the most significant reflection of political developments in the country. The next chapter will examine the agency within the Soviet media system that played the central role in creating social change under Gorbachev—Novosti Press Agency—and consider the historical development of the two most important Novosti publications, *Soviet Life* and *Moscow News*.

3

Soviet Media for a Global Audience

The history of Novosti Press Agency and its two publications gives fundamental insights into the important role the Soviet press played, first as a conservative force under Brehnev, and then as an agitator for social change under Gorbachev. The international press, led by Novosti, was central to Soviet efforts at conveying a carefully planned image abroad.

NOVOSTI PRESS AGENCY
(AGENTSVO PECHATI NOVOSTI—APN)

> If one were to contrast TASS and Novosti in style and tone
> of propaganda and information, one might say that TASS is
> of the Soviet iron age, and Novosti of the nuclear era.
> (Hopkins, 1970:292)

On April 3, 1961, APN was created to supply the world with information about the Soviet Union. Novosti's founding was ordered by Khrushchev in response to TASS's poor performance as an international promoter of Soviet interests. At the founding conference held in February 1961, a report was issued indicating that world interest in the U.S.S.R. had grown markedly, and that it was necessary to "significantly expand and improve information" about the country abroad (*Sovetskaya Pechat,* 3:50). Mark Hopkins (1970) argues that TASS's blatant association with the Soviet government minimized its credibility as a source of objective information, and that TASS's dour, bureaucratic style of journalism would not "sell" the Soviet Union in consumer–oriented markets abroad. According to Hopkins, the solution was to create Novosti, an "unofficial" press agency without direct government ties.

Novosti's founders included leading Soviet "voluntary" organizations: the Union of Journalists, the Union of Writers, the Union of Soviet Societies for Friendship and Cultural Relations with Foreign Countries, and the National Union for the Dissemination of Political and Scientific Knowledge (*Zhurnalist*, 1972:vol.1:5). These organizations inhabit the complex invisible territory between the Communist Party, government, and "unofficialdom." Novosti has been described as "another governmental organ" (Hazan, 1976:43) and "no more divorced from the political establishment than the USIA [United States Information Agency] is in the United States" (Hopkins, 1970:291).

But the issue of what an unofficial agency meant in this context is more complicated. Baruch Hazan tells a more colorful story about Novosti's creation:

> The story begins as far back as 1943, when the German army of Von Paulus surrendered at Stalingrad. Among Von Paulus's officers were several experts in propaganda and disinformation. They were soon discovered by the Soviet authorities, and subsequently utilized during the rest of the war, as well as afterward. In about 1958 the K.G.B. (Komitet Gosudarstvennoi Bezopasnosti—Committee of State Security) organized special courses for propaganda and "disinformation." Among the lecturers were several ex–German experts. Around the end of 1960 the courses were completed. In April 1961 Novosti was created. Many of the graduates from these K.G.B. courses found their place in the newly created "information agency," and today they direct a major part of Novosti's work. Furthermore, according to Western sources the editorial staff of Novosti consists primarily of intelligence officers. One of them is the one–time British agent and Soviet spy, Kim Philby, who later defected to the Soviet Union. (1976:49)

Novosti's three officially declared purposes were: to prepare written and photographic material about Soviet domestic and foreign affairs for the foreign mass media; to supply other Soviet mass media with material on political, economic, scientific, and cultural developments in foreign countries; and to publish magazines, newspapers, and brochures designed to acquaint foreign readers with the Soviet Union (Bogdanov and Vyazemskii, 1966). Novosti can be described as the primary organization responsible for "selling" the Soviet Union to foreign countries, or as one scholar states it, "a public relations agency for the Soviet Union" (Hollander, 1972:32). Despite Novosti's officially unofficial status, it charged only a nominal fee for its services, yet was fully equipped with the necessary technology to carry out many different media tasks. In addition, APN worked through the press departments of many Soviet embassies abroad.

On October 28, 1984, Novosti Press Agency was awarded the Order of the Red Banner of Labor by the U.S.S.R. Supreme Soviet's Presidium "for services in publicizing the domestic and foreign policies of the Communist Party of the Soviet Union and of the Soviet state, and for keeping world opinion informed about the achievements of the Soviet people." The Red Banner Order underscores Novosti's opaquely unofficial status.

Novosti expanded rapidly. In 1964 it established book publishing and television divisions and absorbed Progress Publishers. In 1965 Novosti's clients included 3,500 foreign newspapers and magazines, 70 information agencies, and 80 publishing companies, and in 1967, Novosti had its own representatives in 56 countries as well as 40 established foreign bureaus (Hopkins, 1970).

APN's first chairman, Boris Burkov, remained with the agency until September 1970. In the January 8–14, 1965 issue of the journal *Za Rubezhom* (Abroad) Burkov wrote an overview of his work with the agency. He emphasized that the APN charter stated: "The Soviet state organs are not responsible for the activities, financial obligations, and other actions of Novosti Press Agency." Burkov noted that Novosti materials were used especially by the press in socialist countries, but that Novosti also "enjoyed extensive contacts with Western press organizations." He added that Novosti did not "propose to abandon either its socialist character or its primary task," which was to promote a glamorized vision of the Soviet Union.

By 1972, according to *Zhurnalist*, Novosti's staff was operating in more than 110 countries. It had representatives in 82 countries and connections with 140 major international and national agencies. Between 1965 and 1967 Novosti's book publishing section published over 35 million books, brochures, booklets, albums, and guides in Russian and foreign languages (Ebon, 1987). In 1970 Novosti published 7 newspapers, 50 illustrated magazines, and over 100 information bulletins outside the country. Novosti's photographic department compiled 120,000 photographs yearly, compiling a total collection of more than 2 million. By 1985 APN published in 45 languages in 140 countries, had bureaus in over 70 countries, and had thousands of representatives in many more. The agency had immense power and resources.

Novosti also acted as an intermediary between Western media and Soviet sources, arranging interviews and travel and accompanying visiting journalists. Its web of activities was so broad and complex that even APN heads could not report how many works were in progress at a given moment (Ebon, 1987). Among the best–known publications produced by Novosti in

English were the newspaper *Moscow News*, and the glossy monthly magazine *Soviet Life*.

Novosti's officers moved through a "revolving door" between Novosti, the official press, and the Soviet government and Communist Party. For example, one of the original chairmen of Novosti's Council of Sponsors, Alexei Adzhubei, is also Khrushchev's son-in-law and was formerly chief editor of *Izvestia*. Boris Burkov, who was chairman of the original Novosti board, was deputy chief editor of *Pravda* in 1960 just prior to Novosti's creation. When Burkov retired in 1970, he was replaced as chair by Ivan Udaltsov, who was the minister–counselor at the Soviet embassy during the Soviet military intervention in Czechoslovakia in 1968. Later Udaltsov became deputy director of the Communist Party's Central Committee section on ruling Communist parties (Ebon, 1987). The succeeding Novosti chief Lev Tolkunov was made editor in chief of *Izvestia* in March 1983. He had been on Yuri Andropov's staff in the Central Committee's East European department and had risen to head of that department in 1963. Tolkunov was replaced at Novosti by Pavel Naumov, who also worked in the CPSU Central Committee, at *Pravda* as head of East European affairs, for the periodical *Za Rubezhom* (Abroad), for the monthly *World Marxist Review*, and as editor in chief of *Novoye Vremya* (New Times) (Ebon, 1987).

Novosti became famous as a spy organization with numerous reports of clandestine scandals linked to its staff. John Barron (1974) reported in his book *K.G.B.* that Novosti had a department called "the Tenth Section" that was staffed entirely with K.G.B. officers. He also showed the relationship between double agent Kim Philby (and his compatriot Donald MacLean) and Novosti. Karl Nepomnikhchi, a K.G.B. agent in Vienna in the 1950s, became the first chief editor of Novosti's International Information Editorial Board (Ebon, 1987). Nikolai Borodin, who had a close relationship with Anna Louise Strong, the founder of *Moscow News*, attended a Paris UNESCO conference in 1962 using Novosti press credentials. Borodin earlier worked as the K.G.B.'s Counter-Espionage Director (Seventh Directorate) in 1946 and 1947.

The New York Times reported on March 11, 1966, that Yuri Kuritsin of Novosti was one of a group of journalists expelled from Kenya for "using their positions as a cover for more political activities." In January 1965 Boris Karpovich, a deputy chairman of the Novosti board and an information counselor at the Soviet embassy in Washington, was expelled from the U.S. for spying while he worked at the U.N. Secretariat a few years earlier. Later in 1965 a Soviet journalist working for Novosti reportedly left Oslo, Norway, to have his holiday in the U.S.S.R. just before a spy trial; Novosti's Norway office reported that he would not likely return to Norway (Conquest, 1967). On March 26, 1964, the Guinean government instructed Novosti to stop distributing its bulletins to the public because Novosti was threatening to sever relations between Guinea and other African countries. The following year, the Ceylon Ministry of Defence and External Affairs reported that some Soviet diplomats were publishing notices in Ceylonese newspapers that criticized other countries.

In 1983 the local Novosti chief Aleksei Dumov was deported from Switzerland along with Leonid Ovchinnikov, first secretary at the Soviet embassy and press attaché. The Swiss federal prosecutor Rudolf Friedrich condemned Novosti's Swiss office for "grave interferences in Swiss affairs," and for having "exerted an influence on segments of the Swiss peace movement." In an interview published in the Swiss weekly *Weltwoche* (May 25, 1983), Friedrich claimed that Dumov had been accepted as a journalist and correspondent "to the exclusion of all other activities." He stated:

> Novosti had been assigned the function of a normal press agency, which means that it was to obtain and supply information for the media. But it was never understood that the agency would be a base from which it could interfere in the domestic political opinion–making of Switzerland.

Other Novosti activities included purchasing space in foreign newspapers and sending letters from Novosti correspondents that present the official Soviet perspective. For example, in 1962 a full text of a speech by Khrushchev was placed in several British and Canadian newspapers. One publication, *The Winnipeg Free Press*, asked a Soviet newspaper, *Verchernaya Moskva*, if they would print a notice from the Canadian paper in return; the request was denied (Conquest, 1967).

Historically, Novosti publications have mirrored the mannerisms of the official Soviet press: promoting misinformation, disinformation, and the continuous rewriting of history. People were selectively labelled as either worthy or unworthy of being included in the historical record. When Khrushchev fell from power, a booklet that had just been released in India containing many references to him was quickly recalled and a new one was issued in its place. The new version, "Friendship Visit," never referred to Khrushchev and printed instead the text of an official communique between India and the U.S.S.R., outraging the Indian government (Johnson, 1963). Booklets distributed by Novosti often presented the Soviet Union as though it had no social problems whatsoever. For example, a Novosti booklet entitled "U.S.S.R.: Questions and Answers," answered a question about unemployment by indicating: "We have none."

Gorbachev's policies produced tremendous changes at Novosti. On March 10, 1983, Valentin M. Falin replaced Pavel Naumov as chair of the Novosti board. Naumov went into retirement rather than being moved to another post. Falin is a Russian, was born in 1926 and had been a Communist Party member since 1953. In 1950 he graduated from the Moscow Institute of International Relations and went on to work as a journalist specializing in international affairs. He worked in the Ministry of Foreign Affairs and was Soviet ambassador to West Germany from 1971 to 1978. Falin's work in Germany was described as focused on persuading West Germany to move away from its dependence on the United States (Ebon, 1987:212). Falin served as deputy department head of the Communist Party's Central Committee until 1983. He received three orders of the Red Banner of Labor and the Order of the October Revolution. Falin was the administrator who carried out Gorbachev's directives, including the radical redirection of *Moscow News*. In 1988 Falin left Novosti to become head of the Central Committee's International Department and was replaced by Albert Vlasov, who carried on Falin's reform policies.

Novosti's structural change was evident in its reorganization by a presidential decree in August 1990. Novosti Press Agency was renamed Novosti News Agency, and according to an announcement in *Moscow News*:

> Of course it is not only a change of signboards. Albert Vlasov, former Chairman of the APN Board and now President of N.N.A, told the agency staff that the decree of the USSR President means that the status of an information organization will demand new efforts from its employees since news gathering, processing and distributing will make the N.N.A. work round the clock.
>
> The new status of Novosti increases its responsibility for participating in the elaboration and implementation of the Soviet domestic and foreign policies. This will inevitably entail serious structural changes in the agency. (1990, No. 31:5)

Novosti's evolution demonstrates how political communication both reflects and creates political reality. The Soviet press played a critical role in Soviet society historically and was the vehicle through which changes in the political climate were most clearly reflected (Hollander, 1972:38). Novosti was created for public relations purposes and thus reflects most concisely the symbolic reinventing of the Soviet Union. That reinventing had profound implications for those in the former Soviet Union, as well as for those outside it.

SOVIET LIFE: A GOVERNMENT EXCHANGE

Officially, *Soviet Life* magazine was published in the United States bearing the stamp of the Soviet Embassy, yet it was a Novosti ("unofficial") publication. A reciprocal agreement allowed the U.S. Information Agency to publish the U.S. magazine *America* in the Soviet Union. *Soviet Life* was originally called *USSR*; the name was changed in 1956. In 1961 *Soviet Life* fell under the umbrella of Novosti Press Agency as part of the renewed effort to sell the Soviet Union abroad.

Soviet Life was distinguished by upbeat feature articles and by beautiful pictures of the Soviet Union adorned by smiling beautiful people. There is little of note about the development of *Soviet Life*; as a government initiative, it served the same purpose over three decades of publication—to sanitize Soviet affairs and convince international readers, especially in the United States, that the union was a democracy.

But *Soviet Life* changed with the development of glasnost. According to Sergei F. Ivanko, the magazine's Washington–based editor:

> Our task has always been to present the Soviet Union and its people to the American people ... now that perestroika and glasnost are in full swing, it is much easier for us to present life in the Soviet Union as it is (*The Los Angeles Times*, April 26, 1990:E–6).

The magazine altered its format to resemble Western magazines. In the late 1980s and early 1990's, the magazine examined problems in the Soviet Union, such as alcoholism, overcrowding, insufficient housing, food shortages, and a host of other difficulties. These issues contrast dramatically with the magazine under Brezhnev, which portrayed the Soviet Union without crime, unemployment, or drugs. The history of Novosti's other major publication, *Moscow News*, is more complex and sensational; its origins predate both *Soviet Life* and Novosti.

MOSCOW NEWS: REVOLUTIONARY REPORTING

The *Moscow Daily News* was founded by an American woman, Anna Louise Strong. Strong was a committed leftist who backed the social experiments in the Soviet Union and China and who wanted Americans to see them as something to endorse, not fear. In her travels as a journalist and activist, Ms. Strong:

knew Trotsky well, dined in the White House with Eleanor
and Franklin Roosevelt, and with Stalin's blessing edited the
first English–language newspaper in the Soviet Union. In
the years before 1949 she carried news from Chou En–lai
and Mao Tse–tung to the West, and during the sixties her
Letters from China provided the West with a unique
perspective on Vietnam, the Cultural Revolution and other
major developments in the Far East. (Strong and Keyssar,
1983:viii)

In June 1930 Strong was approached in Moscow by her old friend
Nikolai Borodin, who was later involved in Novosti's clandestine activities in
the1960s. Soviet labor agents had recruited many skilled workers from the
United States to the Soviet Union in 1929 and 1930. Borodin asked Strong if
she had ever thought of developing a newspaper for Americans in Moscow.
Strong had considered the idea for years and decided to accept the task if
Borodin were willing to clear the way in the Soviet Union. The newspaper
began as a vehicle to discuss problems of Americans working in the Soviet
Union and to keep them abreast of U.S. and Soviet developments. It was
written in the livelier style of American journalism, and carried items such as
baseball scores. Strong enthusiastically promoted her newspaper among
noteworthy Americans in Moscow. Joel Shubin, the press officer at the Soviet
Foreign Office, hinted that they might like to adopt the paper (Strong and
Keyssar, 1983).
        The core of the newspaper staff included Strong, Jack Chen, Ed
Falkowski (a Kentucky miner turned writer), Maxwell Stewart (a former
China Outlook editor), and Herbert Marshall (the London Film Guild
secretary). They were soon joined by Millie Mitchell and by Joshua Kunitz, a
writer for the U.S. left publication, *The New Masses*, who was in Moscow to
study theater. Strong worked tirelessly on the paper, typing and laying out
the first paper herself. Her supervisor paid little attention, and the printers
and linotypists could not even read the paper (Strong and Keyssar, 1983).
Her first surprise came when her first issue returned from Glavlit, the
censorship organization. A story that humorously described the problems in
finding an apartment in Moscow was "blue penciled" out and called a
"slander to the Soviet Union" (Strong and Keyssar, 1983).
        The greater shock to Strong came later. After the *Moscow Daily
News'* third week of publication, she left for a lecture tour in the United
States. Not only were her mailed–in articles not printed, but her cables were
not answered. She soon discovered that her supervisor had been replaced by a
man named T. L. Axelrod, and that the newspaper was being filled with
poorly translated and lackluster articles from Russian newspapers. Strong
was too busy with her lecture tour to take any direct action, but was later

assured that when she returned to Moscow her full power as editor would be recognized.

When she returned, however, no one even met Strong at the train station. Her original staff had been replaced by a group of translators and typists, who converted Russian articles into poor English. Her desk had been taken over, and Strong had to work at home. Another English–language newspaper, *The Worker's News*, had been started to answer criticisms that *Moscow News* was too bourgeois. Strong vowed that she would win over the audience by doing a better job, even if *Moscow News* had to look like a Russian paper. According to Strong and Keyssar:

> She started attending all the party congresses and would rush home after an interminable speech to try to scoop *Pravda*. This led to constant conflict with Axelrod, who proved to be a dogmatic ideologue. He insisted on waiting for the official TASS News Agency transcript of each speech and then printing it verbatim. By April 1931 Anna Louise had realized that the real conflict was a double hierarchy. Unbeknownst to her she had a counterpart named Chunak who was also managing editor, but in Russian. She tried to resign "to go to China" for two years, but her resignation went unacknowledged. (1983:154)

In late 1931 Strong took a leave of absence from *Moscow News*. After her many furious complaints, Axelrod was fired, but Strong still did not control the paper. Its new editor, Vascov, was even more of an ideologue. Despite repeated offers to resign, none were accepted, and she was kept on salary and on the masthead even though she never came to the office. Strong made a few efforts to work, such as when she summarized an extremely long speech by Stalin and placed it next to a cartoon by Chen. Vascov instead printed the entire speech and inserted Stalin's picture instead of the cartoon. Vascov asked Strong in anger: "Who is to say what the gist of the great Stalin's speech is?" and she answered: "But, we look just like *Pravda*" (Strong and Keyssar, 1983:156).

Strong wrote a letter to Stalin, hoping to resolve the problem with *Moscow News*. Three days later Stalin's secretary told her the matter was being considered, but Vascov told Strong that her name was being removed from the masthead. Ultimately she had a meeting with Stalin, Vascov, and others:

> With no preliminaries, Stalin spoke to Vascov. "How does it happen that the comrade here complains that you give her no authority, yet insist on retaining her name and call it an

anti–Soviet act if she takes it off? Why is it necessary to use such violence?" Anna Louise thought this meant that Stalin would simply accept the removal of her name from the masthead. But Stalin pressed on: "Would the removal of her name not be a demotion?" Anna Louise was suddenly liberated: "The will that had been dead within me was alive, flaming and free." Quickly and precisely, she explained to him what she wanted. American efficiency could help Russia, but the Soviet Americans needed a newspaper to assist them in their difficult fight to integrate themselves into Russia. There was not a large enough audience to support two separate papers. Stalin interrupted: "Was there not a difference between engineers and workers?" She was momentarily taken aback, then resumed: "American workers and American engineers—all of them in Soviet Russia—are not different enough. They both have the same problems and need one paper to unite them, not two to separate them. We need one good daily." Vacsov caught the direction of the conversation and quickly added his support for "one strong daily." Suddenly, all were agreed. Anna Louise added one final, all–important request, that Nikolai Borodin be named "responsible editor." She, Vacsov and Axelrod would be assistant editors. (Strong and Keyssar, 1983:162)

For a while Strong worked only intermittently with *Moscow News*, since she was busy with another American lecture tour and with writing her autobiography. At the end of March 1934, she returned to Moscow, enthusiastic about working on the paper again. But the newspaper had changed despite her friend Borodin's editorship. It further resembled the patent ideological style of Russian newspapers, in response to what Borodin claimed were the demands of the readers. The political context was also changing: Stalin had initiated the purge trials, and within eighteen months 98 of the 139 members elected to the Central Committee in 1934 had been shot. At the end of October 1936, Anna Louise Strong resigned from the *Moscow News* editorial board (Strong and Keyssar, 1983).

Moscow News maintained its drab format, presenting bureaucratized official news geared toward foreign audiences. With the founding of Novosti Press Agency in 1961, the newspaper fell under that organization's umbrella and was thereafter "officially unofficial." The newspaper continued mimicking the bland, propagandistic style of *Pravda*, *Izvestia*, and other official papers; it was essentially a handout for tourists in Soviet hotels

(Cohen and vanden Heuvel, 1989). But the situation at *Moscow News* changed dramatically under Gorbachev.

GORBACHEV'S *MOSCOW NEWS*

Moscow News served as an important vehicle for social change under Gorbachev, both in the U.S.S.R. and globally. The newspaper was a product and producer of glasnost; under Gorbachev it published stories that would have been labeled heresy under earlier leaders. The newspaper's editor in chief Yegor Yakovlev kept revising the boundaries of the acceptable by consistently but calculatedly moving into previously forbidden journalistic zones. For example, in 1988 *Moscow News* devoted an entire page to resurrected writers Yuli Daniel and Andrei Sinyavsky, who were found guilty under Article 70 of the RSFSR (Russian Soviet Federated Socialist Republic) criminal code ("Agitation or Propaganda conducted with the purpose of undermining or weakening the Soviet government"). Under Brezhnev, Daniel spent five years in a labor camp, and *Izvestia* printed a story about the "malicious renegades." But later in a *Moscow News* interview, Daniel recalled his suppression, and under Gorbachev, his poems and stories began to appear in popular Russian magazines (*Moscow News*, No. 37, Sept. 18–25, 1988).

The press system itself was regularly chided in *Moscow News* for its failure to meet the demands for popular subscriptions. Soviet editors lamented the number of letters to the editor they received as compared with earlier years, claiming they represented the changing relationship between the press and the public. The debate over multiple perspectives was regularly noted in *Moscow News*. For example, an editorial discussed the difference between glasnost and what some referred to as "well intentioned glasnost," which linked freedom of expression to providing good publicity for Gorbachev's policies (*Moscow News* No. 37, Sept. 18–25, 1988).

The editor in chief appointed under Gorbachev, Yegor Yakovlev, had been fired or asked to resign from editorial positions several times during his career. He was fired as deputy editor of *Leninskoe Znamya* and as secretary of the regional Komsomol organization in 1959. In 1966 he was told to resign the position of deputy editor of *Sovietskaya Rossiya,* and from *Komsomolskaya Pravda*. In 1972 he was fired as founding editor of *Zhurnalist* for having an unconventional artist do the cover and some graphics. Yakovlev then went to Prague, but returned to Moscow in 1975 as a feature writer for *Izvestia*. In 1982 when Andropov became General Secretary, Yakovlev was asked to serve as editor of *Izvestia's* department of Communist education, but with Chernenko's succession, he quit and went back to Prague to avoid his previous employment problems (Cohen and vanden Heuvel:1989).

In August 1985, shortly after Gorbachev became general secretary, Yakovlev was offered the position as *Moscow News* editor in chief by Valentin Falin, the head of Novosti Press Agency. Falin explained that the newspaper was to be unique, publishing what other Soviet newspapers would not publish and reflecting the true spirit of glasnost. Yakovlev accepted the job despite his (and his wife's) fears that he would "end up with his bare ass on the sidewalk again" (Cohen and vanden Heuvel, 1989:199). While some have suggested that Yakovlev himself was a conformist in his strict adherence to Lenin, Yakovlev actually claimed that the U.S.S.R. had to move beyond Leninism, with glasnost, public opinion, and democratization. The Soviet Union was, in his opinion, ready for these changes now, unlike in Lenin's time (Cohen and vanden Heuvel, 1989).

Even though the phrase "*Moscow News*—The Flagship of Perestroika" was used in a 1987 advertisement, Yakovlev rejected the analogy as immodest and inaccurate. *Pravda* and *Izvestia,* the official newspapers, had much larger circulations (in the millions); measured in terms of availability, they had a greater public impact. But *Moscow News,* with a circulation of only about 350,000 copies in Russia and about 1.2 million worldwide, sold for outrageous prices on the black market. Customers would often rent the newspaper, reading and returning it so that it could be leased out again.

Yakovlev claims he had two goals when he became editor in chief of *Moscow News* in 1986. First he wanted to give what was basically a tourist newspaper a "real political identity" (Cohen and vanden Heuvel, 1989:202). This meant covering topics that other newspapers avoided. Second, he wanted to establish ties with other nations, to break down stereotypes about the Soviet Union abroad, and to break down stereotypes within the U.S.S.R. about the West. Yakovlev claims he did not try to make *Moscow News* into a Western newspaper, but rather into a Soviet newspaper that would critically assess Soviet society and policies. He told his reporters to "write for the paper as they talk at home," so that "each new issue is like an oar rowing us farther and farther from the joyless past we are leaving behind" (Cohen and vanden Heuvel, 1989:203).

When Yakovlev took over *Moscow News,* he fired and replaced about 60 staff people. Many other writers contributed to the paper besides staff members, and Yakovlev spent a great deal of time talking with potential contributors. Under Yakovlev's editorial arrangement, he was responsible for all decisions, whereas with other newspapers, such as *Pravda* and *Izvestia,* the editor had to submit a final draft to the editorial board for approval. A representative from Glavlit had an office at *Moscow News* headquarters, according to an account by Yakovlev.

> His name is Misha, and his office is near mine. He reads the
> contents of the upcoming issue. He's not very bright, but
> he's a sweet and mild–mannered fellow—just a regular guy.
> All he can do is object that something might disclose
> military or state secrets. Or to something pornographic, but
> we don't have any of that in *Moscow News*. He or his own
> superior can say to me, "Aren't you worried about this
> article for this or that reason?" Sometimes they are right
> and occasionally I correct something, but they can't forbid
> me to publish something. I can say, "Thanks for your
> opinion, but I'll make the decision" (Cohen and vanden
> Heuvel, 1989:204).

The process of glasnost steadily reduced the forbidden "zones" or
topics that the press could not cover. *Moscow News* was at the forefront of
this movement toward greater press freedom. Yakovlev saw journalism come
a long way in just a few years. For example, in 1987 he had a reprint of a
letter written by two writers expelled from the Soviet writers union pulled
from the paper at the last moment, forcing him to delay the paper to fill the
space. The *Moscow News* office was deluged with calls from readers asking for
an explanation that could not be given. By 1990, however, Yakovlev claimed
that "*Moscow News* just wouldn't give in to that kind of pressure" (Cohen
and vanden Heuvel, 1989:205). While the editor might not give in, he
nevertheless faced stark criticism from both above and below. But both
Georgi Arbatov and Valentin Falin, who left Novosti in the fall of 1988 to
head the Central Committee's International Department, gave Yakovlev
political assistance in tenuous times. In 1989 Yakovlev was elected to the
Congress of People's Deputies, which strengthened his position on issues of
glasnost. He was elected from the radical filmmakers union, rather than the
more conservative journalists union, which, according to Yakovlev, "is still
dominated by utterly untalented people from the provinces" (Cohen and
vanden Heuvel, 1989:208). Yakovlev described his view on being an editor as
follows:

> It is not enough just to be courageous. You have to be brave
> in a professional way. A real editor has to walk along the
> edge of the abyss if his newspaper is to play a useful, positive
> role, but he must protect his paper by not going over the
> edge of the abyss. That is hard to do. Every day you have to
> grope for the political openings and possibilities. It is very
> hard to walk along the edge of this abyss.
>   What it means is that good editors will make good
> newspapers and bad editors will make bad ones. And the

bad newspapers will be punished by their readers.
Newspapers and magazines that have embraced glasnost
have soaring subscriptions. But look at the newspaper *Trud*.
Once it had the largest circulation and was gaining
subscribers regularly. Then it started losing readers because
it wasn't dealing with urgent, topical issues. Glasnost ought
to be the golden age for Soviet newspapers, as it is for our
journals (Cohen and vanden Heuvel, 1989:209).

Yakovlev viewed himself as part of the struggle for progressive
journalism, which in turn, promoted the success of perestroika. He echoed
Gorbachev's call for greater tolerance in listening to opposing points of view.
As a result, he broadened *Moscow News'* coverage of everyday life and of the
workers. He claimed that glasnost and perestroika would benefit the workers
as well as the intelligentsia, arguing that the conservative forces in the Soviet
Union had "nothing positive to offer the country" (Cohen and vanden
Heuvel, 1989:212).

In August of 1990, Yegor Yakovlev made a plea to readers. He
announced that Novosti Press Agency would no longer provide any printing
facilities or infrastructure for the *Moscow News* staff. APN had recently
declared that *Moscow News* must be allowed to publish through its own
efforts. For the next year the Soviet government ensured only seventy percent
of the previous year's circulation. Yakovlev claimed that conservatives in the
CPSU Central Committee had "systematically infringed on the interests of
this publication," (p. 6) ignoring the demands of readers for more copies of
the paper. The newspaper thus became a "moonshine publication," available
only on the black market. In response to these pressures, Yakovlev
announced the following measures:

1. Subscriptions for the 1991 Russian–language edition of
    MN were announced, with a plea to readers and
    workers at paper mills and printing and publishing
    centers for help.
2. The newspaper was transferred to joint stock principles,
    with measures taken to promote readers as the main
    shareholders.
3. A *Moscow News* international information center was
    to be created in cooperation with international
    newspapers and magazines.
4. Russian–language editions of foreign papers would be
    sponsored by *Moscow News* to end the one–way nature
    of the East–West bridge. The first would be released in

> September, when *Moscow News* would put out an issue
> of the French magazine *Paris Match* for Soviet readers.

In this same issue, minutes of a roundtable discussion about the future of *Moscow News* were also released. Discussants agreed that the newspaper's boldness must be preserved, while objectivity, verified facts, fairness, honesty, respect for opposing views, and internal criticism were also included among the paper's objectives. While the paper should rise above any political forces, it was nonetheless seen as playing a critical role on the "left flank of the struggle unfolding in society" (*Moscow News*, August 5–12, 1990). The discussion ended with a call to readers for their recommendations.

On August 7, 1990, allegedly the last censorship seals were placed on Soviet publications, and Glavlit was removed from the Soviet press system. But a *Moscow News* commentary argued that although formal censorship was no longer in place, words and thoughts were still far from being free (1990, No. 31), since the prevailing Communist party leadership remained in charge of the press. Soon after, censorship was reinstated, at first through covert measures advanced by the Party, and then by a decree of temporary reinstatement.

A comparative–historical analysis of these Novosti publications—*Soviet Life* and *Moscow News*—will demostrate the process by which the media forms as well as the image of the Soviets were transformed under Gorbachev. We must first understand the image of the "old Soviets" and the framing of the Soviet Union prior to Gorbachev. In the next chapter we will examine the Soviet national image that *Soviet Life* presented under Brezhnev. We will focus on the years 1972 to1974, at the height of Brezhnev's power in Soviet society.

4

Heaven on Earth: *Soviet Life* under Brezhnev

What was the image that *Soviet Life* gave Americans of Soviet society? What kind of magazine was it, how did it differ from U.S. publications, and what characterized the content? This chapter addresses these questions.

THE FORMAT AND STYLE OF *SOVIET LIFE*

The sentence structure and word complexity of the U.S. print media are relatively simple. Paragraphs are generally three sentences long, sentences generally use less than twenty words, and words over two syllables are avoided (Tuchman, 1978:106). Articles in *Soviet Life* were notably complex by these standards. Each issue contained at least one highly technical or scientific article, which outlined very specialized academic findings. The magazine also presented substantial Marxist–Leninist political theory unfamiliar to the average American. Sentences commonly included many words with more than three syllables; many of them, such as "dialectical materialism" and "imperialism," are not in common usage in the United States. For example, a sentence from the November 1972 "Editor's Notes" section reads: "A simplistic extrapolation of the existing phenomena of bourgeois society features all the negative aspects of the present industrial system of capitalism as though they were absolutes" (*Soviet Life*, November 1972:3).

Articles in *Soviet Life* were regularly reprinted from *Pravda, Izvestia,* and other official Soviet publications, underscoring the transparency of Novosti's officially unofficial status. Why would the magazine rely so heavily on those official publications if it were truly an independent magazine?

THE MAGAZINE'S AUDIENCE

Reading *Soviet Life* could easily mislead a reader as to its intended audience. The magazine was presented as a publication for the average American citizen, but the content was mixed. The letters to the editor printed in each issue purportedly came from common American citizens, often from small towns. In these letters readers generally thanked the editor for information about the U.S.S.R., about which they otherwise would not have had balanced information. Was this a magazine for the "lay" public? While some features were appropriate for an unspecialized audience, others, such as those on different geographic regions and cultural matters, seem directed toward members of American academia. Still another portion of the magazine seemed intended for members of the U.S. polity, with repeated references to disputes between the U.S. and Soviet governments, denunciations of American policies, and responses to criticism from Richard Nixon's political administration. Thus, it appeared that the magazine attempted to reach several different categories of Americans: citizen, scientist, and politician.

THE MAGAZINE'S COVERAGE

Several journalists wrote regularly throughout this time period of *Soviet Life*. Many articles were written by Soviet scientists who specialized in the academic area covered. Articles were often written by journalists explicitly employed by the official press. Other articles included interviews of government and academic figures and Soviet citizens. Most of the political commentary was written by Spartak Beglov, but he was also joined by Vladimir Pozner and Gennadi Gerasimov, who later became the two most prominent Soviet journalists. Much of the "academic" material was also political, legitimating the Soviet social system or reporting the successes of socialism. As an example of this, Soviet Foreign Minister Andrei Gromyko's son, Anatoli Gromyko, wrote for *Soviet Life* as a historian discussing the prospects for U.S.–Soviet cooperation and détente.

Two people were featured in every issue of *Soviet Life* during this time period: Vladimir I. Lenin and Leonid I. Brezhnev. The only exception was the September 1972 issue, in which there was no mention of Brezhnev. While the specific actors who played the remaining characters changed, the primary cast of noted figures remained essentially the same. The secondary cast of unknown people legitimated the magazine's presentation of Soviet life.

THE PRIMARY CAST

The primary cast included authority figures who framed the publication's content based on their access to power—either political or intellectual. The first cast member was the editor himself. Throughout this period, the editor in chief was Alexander L. Makarov, Washington editor was Anatoly A. Mkrtchian, and managing editor was Nikolai P. Popov. While the reader was not given information about the editor, and he never signed his editorial comments, the "Editor's Notes" section near the front of the magazine set the stage for the remaining contents. In this section various Soviet policies were set forth, which were then illustrated as being democratic and successful by the features in that issue.

The second group of authority figures included the two sacred leaders, Lenin and Brezhnev. While obviously more prestigious than the editor, their speeches or writings were used nonetheless to validate the publication's content. Lenin and Brezhnev were written about, rather than actively writing themselves.

The third group of authority figures consisted of Soviet government officials. Every issue included a number of articles written by various Communist Party officials and members of the U.S.S.R. Supreme Soviet. The fourth group of contributors in the primary cast were the academicians who, as the representative intellectuals, served as "mouthpieces" for the merits of Soviet social, political, and economic behavior. They also forecasted future Soviet development in unerringly positive terms.

The final group in the primary cast included authority figures from the West: prominent Americans who had visited the U.S.S.R. and were interviewed or featured in *Soviet Life* and quoted on their positive impressions of the Soviet Union. These characters included U.S. governors, prominent businesspersons and trade representatives, and mayors of large American cities.

THE SECONDARY CAST

The secondary cast legitimatized the discourse of the primary cast by way of example. It included "model" Soviet citizens of many stripes. The first type was the worker: Every issue devoted significant attention to the hard working citizen who worked for the job's intrinsic satisfaction and from a sense of duty to the Soviet state rather than the pursuit of material gain. All kinds of workers appeared in *Soviet Life*. Often they were featured in relationship to industrial progress and depicted as heroes who were bringing communism to life.

The second type of model citizen was the responsible youth. Youths were also workers, but they were especially notable for their enormous pride and responsibility and for their many accomplishments. The third kind of model citizen was the elderly man or woman who had fought for Bolshevism, survived World War II (and perhaps the loss of spouse or family), and was still a dedicated patriot working for the common good.

The fourth model citizen type was the common denizen who also served as a deputy to the Supreme Soviet. This character is depicted as an average worker, who is nonetheless represented in government because of his or her extraordinary dedication and leadership potential. For example, the May 1972 issue featured a male house painter who was a deputy to the U.S.S.R. Supreme Soviet. This focus allowed the Soviet government to be depicted as truly representing the common laborer.

The fifth type of model citizen was the superwoman. She was shown to be liberated, as she had equal or superior stature to men in her field of employment. Women from occupations where they were underrepresented in the West were often featured, such as women test pilots, engineers, and politicians. These women were also shown as devout wives and mothers who managed to have both a career and family.

Often these model citizen categories were combined, so that *Soviet Life* would perhaps feature a young male university student who was a member of parliament (November 1972); an elderly woman who lost her husband in the "Great Patriotic War" (World War II) and who now headed a collective farm as well as being a deputy to the Supreme Soviet, or twenty-year-olds who ran the Volga auto plant (March 1973).

THE MAGAZINE'S SETTINGS

Each issue emphasized a geographic region and a technological problem. These themes were tied together as in the January 1974 issue where the focus was on Siberia and on oil drilling. The sociopolitical theme of the issue may or may not have been related to former themes: In the January 1974 issue, a Brezhnev speech at an international peace conference was printed along with political commentary by Spartak Beglov criticizing U.S. military intervention abroad, particularly in Vietnam.

The geographic setting staged articles in each issue, except those dealing with political issues. Generally, the "Soviet People" section contained articles on people in the chosen region; the "Literature and the Arts" section detailed music, art, dance, and literature from the area; and the "Economy and Science" section addressed economic and scientific developments in the same geographic area. The magazine also contained attractive pictures of the area's natural resources, its cities, and its smiling people.

MEDIA FRAMES

The Soviet image presented in *Soviet Life* relied on creating an unswervingly favorable view of the Soviet Union for the Western readers. The content of *Soviet Life* under Brezhnev was organized around five media "frames," or organizing packages: 1. the effectiveness of socialism, 2. Soviet democracy, 3. the cooperative Soviets, 4. the Soviet foreign policy highground, and 5. the hail–Lenin frame.

The Effectiveness of Socialism

Soviet Life presented an untarnished image of Soviet socialism in terms of the economy, education, health care, technology and industrial development, environmental issues, and public happiness. According to Soviet sociologists, the communist future was not far away (January 1972). Socialism had provided, particularly for people in the non–Russian republics, the opportunity to advance at a rate not possible prior to their voluntary incorporation into the U.S.S.R. The Union of Soviet Socialist Republics was depicted as a completely cooperative arrangement where all citizens benefited from the benevolence of the Soviet peoples. In 1972 the president of each Republic affirmatively answered the question: "What event, what fact in the life of your republic, is most characteristic of the friendship of the Soviet peoples?" (January 1972).

Uzbekistan was shown making tremendous gains in every sphere since the October Revolution. The rate of literacy was said to have increased to allow Uzbekistan to go ahead of the West in education. People were also shown to own and control the means of production, the yield of cotton was higher, hunger and poverty had been eradicated, and the creation of a working class was now complete. Literature and the arts were reported as flourishing, along with advancing industrialization and work specialization (May 1972).

The same advancements were reported in Turkmenistan, Tajikistan, Kirghizia, Estonia, Azerbaijan, Georgia, Latvia, Lithuania, Ukraine, and Siberia in the R.S.F.S.R. These reviews were supplemented by predictions by Soviet politicians and economists about future economic conditions. For example, the Azerbaijan S.S.R. (Soviet Socialist Republic) chairman of the Council of Ministers claimed that during the next five–year plan (1971–1975), real per capita income would grow by thirty–three percent (September 1972). Johannes Kebin, first secretary to the Estonian Communist Party's Central Committee, noted that during the same five–year plan, labor productivity in Estonia would grow by thirty–six percent in industry and construction, and by thirty–one percent in agriculture, while real per capita income would grow by twenty–four–and–a–half percent.

Cooperation among republics was emphasized as well. According to Kebin:

> What is the groundwork for our ambitious plan? The friendship and mutual assistance of all the peoples of the U.S.S.R. Estonia's achievements are a product of the joint efforts of all the fraternal republics ... To put it simply, the cooperation of different nationalities is a mighty booster of social progress. This cooperation, based on the equality of the fraternal republics, is the reality behind the target figures of our five–year plan. (July 1972:46)

Givi Dzhavakhishvili, chairman of the Council of Ministers of the Georgian S.S.R. concurred in the September 1972 issue. In the same issue, the 1970 Census was cited to testify that "returns show that nations and nationalities of the Soviet Union have freely chosen the Russian language for mutual communication" (p. 35). The issue of relations between different national groups was frequently addressed. In one article entitled "How the National Question is Being Solved in the U.S.S.R." (September 1972), Lenin's policies about the importance of full equality for people regardless of their nationality were outlined. Lenin was cited 16 times in this two–page article. In a November 1972 article entitled "The U.S.S.R.: 50 Years Old— Creating a Union of Free Republics," each republic was portrayed as being self–determined, based on Lenin's principle of peaceful coexistence; Lenin was referenced 23 times in two pages. According to a December 21, 1972, report by Leonid Brezhnev on the fiftieth anniversary of the U.S.S.R., the national question had been solved "fully, ultimately, and irrevocably" (March 1973:34).

The Soviet economy was presented as not only rapidly developing at each regional level, but as being perfectly synchronized at the national level. According to the editor:

> Since we do not have any private capitalist property, nor, therefore, any clashes of contradictory interests, we have been able to create a well–balanced economy that can be compared to a well–coordinated orchestra. Just as there are no unnecessary instruments in a good orchestra so there are no unnecessary parts in a sound economy. We have no falling off of production, and therefore, no unemployment. (March 1973:3)

Unemployment was portrayed in *Soviet Life* as nonexistent, or as one issue stated, "an extinct concept." According to the author Konstantin Suvorov, Candidate of Science in History:

> Socialism and joblessness are economic polar opposites. Planning plus collectivized farming and industrialization ended unemployment in the Soviet Union forty years ago. By 1930 the last labor exchange was closed—it was no longer needed. An entire generation has been born, raised, and come to maturity in a society without crises and depressions, while other countries were experiencing their periodic booms and busts. (September 1973:43)

Soviet socialism was also represented as providing an excellent education for all and as giving freedom of choice to citizens in their careers. In the May 1973 edition the "Editor's Notes" section addressed formal education and the school experience. The reader was told that education was free of charge in the U.S.S.R., that there were no privileged or underprivileged classes, and that young people had a "civic responsibility and drive to learn the hard way" (p. 3), by traveling to faraway places to work on projects for the country. In this sense, education did not mimic the narrow pragmatism that was imputed to the West.

Education was booming in all contexts, according to *Soviet Life*, so that almost everyone was enrolled in some type of formal education. Schools were shown to be changing rapidly to keep up with the scientific progress in the nation. In addition, Soviet citizens were portrayed as avid readers. The March 1972 issue described Muscovites as voracious readers; one Muscovite among many interviewed in the September 1972 issue, claimed he had "a small library of 500–600 books" (p. 49).

Complete freedom of choice was said to exist for students to pick their occupations since tuition was free and students received stipends. However, full–time technical and higher school graduates had to work three years on jobs they were assigned. According to the editor: "One should keep in mind that the state has spent considerable funds on the training of specialists and has the right to expect at least partial compensation" (March 1973:3). Soviet teachers were shown as being well supported by the state, such as when Soviet teachers were reported to be given temporary jobs and free housing when a dramatic decrease in the need for primary school teachers occurred following World War II.

The way the state met the public's health needs was also a prominent theme in *Soviet Life*. Free medical services were discussed in terms of socialist advances in each republic. In the September 1972 issue, the "Editor's Notes" section, entitled "Free Medical Care for All," outlined the ways socialism has met people's medical needs. An article appeared in the same issue about two American doctors who visited the Soviet Union and were very impressed with the ambulance services. According to the magazine:

> It is an unqualified fact that any citizen in our country can have the best medical care, consultation with top specialists, the most complicated operation and inpatient treatment of any duration. There is no charge for any of this. (September 1972:3)

Furthermore, the editor argued, such an arrangement was possible only in a planned economy. Medical professions were said to be honored in the Soviet Union, and salaries of all medical workers had recently been raised.Technology, science, and industry were shown to be advancing rapidly in the Soviet Union. *Soviet Life* often included complex academic research findings unsuited for a general audience. For example, the January 1972 issue featured an article by a biophysicist on heliobiology. In the September 1972 issue, an article appeared by a scientist studying "flashing stars." The March 1973 issue featured a piece on plant genetics. In the May 1972 issue, a relationship between the natural and social sciences was posited, claiming that "real progress in science is impossible without a materialistic view of the world" (p. 35). Environmental destruction was portrayed as nonexistent under socialism as well. The editor stated:

> The optimism of Soviet scientists is based on the fact that theirs is a socialist society in which land is nationalized and economic development is planned. These are the two conditions necessary to ensure that technical progress is no threat to the environment. (July 1972:14)

Soviet Life regularly featured articles that emphasized the cleanliness of Soviet cities, the tending of green space, and various conservation efforts. Generally these articles were accompanied by beautiful pictures that suggested that Soviet land remain pure. An article on Moscow's pollution inspector was placed next to a photo of the city with a rainbow over it. The city was said to be kept clean simply by moving the most polluting factories outside the city limits. Crime was also said to be rare; *Soviet Life* stated that crime in the U.S.S.R. had almost been eliminated, while crime in capitalist countries was up by sixty–five percent (March 1972). In addition, the criminal justice system was said to be very efficient and fair, albeit unnecessary.

According to *Soviet Life*, the conditions created by Soviet socialism, which included a balanced economy, a government of the people, free education and health care, full employment, and almost no crime or pollution, allowed the development of a "new Soviet citizen" (March 1972); thus, throughout *Soviet Life* the model citizen was portrayed as a natural adjunct to a model society. According to an Uzbekistan Communist Party official and member of the Supreme Soviet (May 1972), the new person molded by socialism was characterized by a sense of social duty, a pride in industry, and an awareness of the personal responsibility the individual had for the national common good. This citizen understood that he or she was obligated to work for the "socialist homeland" and the Communist Party.

The model citizen types provided evidence of this phenomenon. Dedicated workers, socially responsible youth, and superwomen gave testimony to the editor's notion that the consumer in the West could not determine his or her future because of the improper socioeconomic conditions:

> Socialist society creates these conditions. It is the perfect medium for developing the human personality. The entire experience of socialist construction irrefutably proves that human desires do not grow quantitatively but improve qualitatively, shifting to predominantly cultural values. When Soviet sociologists say there is no limit to human desires, they mean there is no limit to the perfection of man and the ennoblement of the pattern of his requirements. (November 1972:3)

Public ownership of the means of production, according to the editor, promoted the development of the human being. A special magazine section was devoted to Soviet workers: "people who created the material values but do not have the narrow materialist approach to life." Accordingly, "the ideals of the party, the ideals of communism, have become for such a worker the essence of his entire outlook" (November 1972:3,5).

Soviet Democracy

The Soviet social system, according to *Soviet Life*, functioned as a democracy under Brezhnev. The system was portrayed as humanitarian, fair, and devoid of any type of racial, ethnic, gender, or religious discrimination, with equal opportunity for all citizens, and no human rights violations.

The idea that leaders were elected proved a major theme in the March 1972 issue. An article entitled "Representing the People" described a Moscow City Soviet deputy who received a majority (ninety–nine percent) of the votes. The article failed to note that he was the only candidate. The same was true of the U.S.S.R. Supreme Soviet deputy, who was featured in a piece titled "Elected by the People, Responsible to Them." The issue also carried an essay titled "What is Soviet Power?" which contended that, consistent with Lenin, the origin of the Soviet government was the people, and that: "The new state power was an authority open to all; it carried out all its functions before the eyes of the masses, was accessible to the masses, of their will" (p. 10).

An essay entitled "Democracy in the Soviet Union: What it Means and How it Works," emphasized that the guaranteed right to work, freedom from exploitation, and unemployment were the bedrocks of democracy. Additional elements of Soviet democracy were the collective ownership of the means of production, freedom of speech, freedom of the press, and freedom of assembly and public organization. Stocks of paper and printing presses were said to be "at the disposal of working people." Anyone could criticize the social system, according to *Soviet Life*, and *Pravda* would print their comments: "No Soviet citizen can be brought to court for criticizing ... for his thoughts and convictions" (March 1972:17); national and racial equality were said to be guaranteed.

As *Soviet Life* outlined the "advancement of Socialist democracy" the Soviet Union was portrayed as becoming even more democratic. Greater participation was shown in "public" institutions, and in economic and political life (trade unions). An essay on retirement noted that pensions for the aged were "all free, of course" (p. 26); another declared that citizens had absolute freedom of worship, and the separation of church and state in the Soviet Union was held up as proof that religion was "a private affair" (p. 29); further, to deny a Soviet citizen his or her rights based on religious beliefs was a crime. Finally, that issue detailed the "People's Control," an inspection system designed to monitor business corruption and the quality of consumer goods.

According to the editor, a new law passed in relation to the deputies to the Soviets showed the advanced development of socialist democracy. He argued that "The deputy is guided by the mandate of the electorate and by public opinion, which he constantly sounds out." He added that in 1971, 197 deputies to local Soviets were stripped of their powers due to "a loss of confidence by the voters or actions by the deputy that make him unworthy of his office" (January 1973:3).

Soviet Life emphasized the important human rights available to all Soviet citizens, such as the right to work, a place to live, electoral participation, human dignity, family and property rights, and copyright and inheritance rights. *Soviet Life* claimed that women were not excluded from Soviet democracy, as changes in the status of women were among the crowning achievements of socialism. The May 1972 "Editor's Notes" section titled "Women in Politics, Women in the Arts," detailed how, particularly in the Central Asian republics, women had been elevated from second–class citizenship to complete equality with men. An interview (reprinted from *Zhurnalist)* of Lydia Lirvinenko, a science candidate in economics, and senior scientific worker for the State Committee for Labor Resources of the Council of Ministers of the Russian Federation, argued that women should not quit working after having children since that would make them feel useless (March 1972).

Another woman author discussed changes in the status of women in Tajikistan in a piece titled "Freed of the Black Veil" (May 1972). The writer, located in Leninabad, wrote of the amazing progress women had made since the October Revolution. She noted that women were still loving wives and mothers, even with their work responsibilities. Women in Soviet society were said to monopolize the fields of medicine and education and to be guaranteed work and comparable worth.

A piece that addressed questions from American readers about Soviet women (with no reference as to who made the inquiries) addressed the questions: Why do Soviet women work? Do men and women get equal pay for equal work? and, Are Soviet women doing "double duty?" The response to the third question was that, yes, women in the Soviet Union were doing both paid labor and nonpaid domestic work; but some solutions were proposed. None of them, however, included greater participation by husbands in domestic work. Instead it was suggested that the state provide child care and that the woman relinquish her work upon the birth of the first child. In response to the question "Doesn't femininity disappear when women work?" *Soviet Life* answered: "Our women, independent though they are, are still women. They prize their femininity and their appeal, just like women the world over" (March 1973:20).

According to *Soviet Life,* Jews also occupied a high status position in the U.S.S.R., although they were said to be rapidly assimilating into the general population. No discrimination was said to exist, as "In the Soviet Union, a man's success in life depends on his knowledge, abilities, industry, and attitude toward people. His nationality or race mean nothing" (July 1972:53). In a July 1973 article entitled "Who Runs the State?," the magazine argued that all nationalities and categories of people govern the nation. The majority of deputies to the Supreme Soviet were reported to be farmers, with over half of them under the age of 30.

An article called "The CPSU and the Leadership of Society" addressed the question: "Isn't a one–party system a contradiction of democracy?" The answer was no, according to *Soviet Life*: "The point is not the number of parties, but whose interests they protect." The article suggested that even in societies where many parties existed, they may only represent one group and therefore not be democratic. Communist Party leadership was not "something imposed from without;" instead, it was "fully democratic and independent. Soviet public organizations voluntarily accept the leading role of the Communist Party" (November 1973:5). Lenin's name appeared ten times in this piece.

The Cooperative Soviets

Soviet Life regularly carried features that underscored the importance of cooperation between East and West, between the Soviet Union and the United States, on political, economic, ecological, scientific, and cultural matters. The May 1972 issue examined Antarctica as a "model of cooperation," in which many nations had jointly explored the area. Soviet Life called this "the greatest peacetime activity in man's history" (p. 47).

The same issue carried an article entitled "For Mutual Understanding," which overviewed the second annual conference of the Institute of Soviet–American relations at Friendship House in Moscow. The institute was reportedly founded in 1962 "on the initiative of the Soviet public," since "the Soviet people have repeatedly shown their readiness to cooperate with the people of the U.S. in the interests of both countries and to work for universal peace" (May 1972:2). Conference participants included Georgi Arbatov, who was then the director of the U.S.A./Canada Institute. United States governors who visited the Soviet Union were also featured in the May 1972 edition. Each governor's comments about the visit were printed in Soviet Life; all of them were positive. An article in the same issue entitled "On a Promising Path" (p. 44) discussed the possibilities for trade and economic agreements between the two nations, and their cooperation in fighting cardiovascular diseases was featured in the November 1973 issue. The magazine claimed there was great interest in U.S. history in the U.S.S.R., so that occasional pieces recognizing Thomas Edison and Benjamin Franklin were run and a symposium on American studies was covered in the July 1972 issue.

A delegation from the U.S. United Auto Workers Union visited the U.S.S.R., as did a delegation from the United Electrical, Radio, and Machine Workers of America. Quotes from members of these groups about how impressed they were with Soviet technology and society were presented in Soviet Life along with features on the meetings between unionists. The July 1973 issue covered the development of the first U.S./U.S.S.R. sister cities arrangement between Tashkent and Seattle; Soviet Life reported that during the visit of Soviets from Tashkent to the United States, The National Enquirer interviewed Soviet astrophysicists regarding their research on extraterrestrials.

Authority figures featured prominently in the "cooperative frame." For example, the cover of the July 1972 issue pictured Richard Nixon and Leonid Brezhnev shaking hands, and the magazine carried copies of several documents signed by the two leaders during the Moscow summit. The "Basic

Principles of Relations between the Union of Soviet Socialist Republics and the United States of America," signed May 29, 1972, by Nixon and Brezhnev, set forth twelve principles of agreement between the two leaders. The document claimed there was no alternative to peaceful coexistence in a nuclear age; therefore, the two superpowers should avoid conflict and promote peace internationally. To prevent military conflicts and the outbreak of nuclear war, the document claimed that the two leaders would be certain that agreements were implemented, that high level exchanges continued, and that armaments were continually limited. In addition, the two countries were to further develop commercial and economic ties, to further science and technology exchanges, cultural ties, and tourism, and to institutionalize these contacts. Both leaders agreed to recognize the sovereignty of all states, although a final caveat noted that this document did not affect previous obligations of either the Soviet Union or the United States to other nations.

In the same issue, Nixon and Brezhnev were pictured signing a treaty limiting anti–ballistic missile systems on May 26, 1972. A joint Soviet–American communique outlined several areas in which the two countries should cooperate, including those listed above, and on procedures for maritime activities (to avoid accidents), and on space exploration. On international issues, the leaders expressed a need to cooperate in Europe: to recognize territorial integrity, the inviolability of frontiers, noninterference in internal affairs of nations, sovereign equality, independence, and the renunciation of the use or threat of force. These measures were to be the basis of détente, according to the communique. The document stated that both the Soviet Union and the United States supported the arrangement of a conference on security and cooperation in Europe and a reciprocal reduction of arms in Central Europe.

Both leaders affirmed their support for a peaceful settlement of Middle East conflicts. They congratulated themselves on achievements in arms control and promised to continue efforts to curb chemical weapons. Their stated goal was to end the arms race, with complete disarmament as the ultimate goal. Both Nixon and Brezhnev expressed their desire to strengthen the United Nations through strict observance of the U.N. Charter and continued bilateral cooperation and meetings. Finally, President Nixon invited General Secretary Brezhnev and Chairman of the U.S.S.R. Council of Ministers Alexei Kosygin to the United States for the next meeting.

Brezhnev's visit to the United States was covered in the September 1973 edition, with a cover photograph of Brezhnev smiling and smoking a cigarette. The issue carried the text of an address by the general secretary to the American people, which emphasized that the Soviet Union was a peace–loving country. The address reiterated the themes of the earlier summit, including the prevention of nuclear war and peaceful coexistence. *Soviet Life* reported that the Soviet people unanimously supported Brezhnev's actions during the summit and believed that the Cold War had begun to thaw.

Prominent Americans were also interviewed in the November 1973 issue on their thoughts about the agreements between Nixon and Brezhnev. Gennadi Gerasimov interviewed J. William Fulbright, then chairman of the Senate Foreign Relations Committee; John Connally, former governor of Texas; Fred Seed, president of Cargill (a major corporation); Cyrus Eaton, industrialist and banker; and Peter Peterson, former U.S. secretary of commerce and then chairman of the Board of Lehman Brothers. All of these men expressed their confidence in the agreements between the Soviet and U.S. leaders.

The Soviet Foreign Policy Highground

Soviet Life presented the Soviets as taking the foreign policy high ground, and conveyed foreign policy differences with the West—especially hostility to the United States and/or capitalism. The discourse of conflict was often embedded in official speeches and academic articles; opposition to the West was communicated both directly and indirectly.

The most recurrent issue within this frame concerned differences between the United States and the Soviet Union about Vietnam. Even within the context of President Nixon's visit to the U.S.S.R., which on the whole was presented as a watershed in improving bilateral relations, the two leaders expressed differing views on Indochina. In the document, "Basic Principles of Relations between the Union of Soviet Socialist Republics and the United States," printed in the July 1972 issue of *Soviet Life*, Nixon claimed that the conflict had to end soon. He noted that North Vietnam should return all Americans held captive in the region. Nixon argued for an internationally supervised cease fire, after which U.S. troops would be withdrawn over a four month period. In addition, the United States would be willing to negotiate with North Vietnam. The view expressed by General Secretary Brezhnev was in solidarity with "the just struggle of the peoples of Laos, Cambodia, and Vietnam" (July 1972:7). Brezhnev called on the United States to cease the bombings of Vietnam and to withdraw all troops so that the Vietnamese could determine their own fate.

Also in the July 1972 issue, an anonymous commentary on the summit appeared. It discussed how the "Soviet people" interpreted the summit: as the next step toward implementing the Soviet peace plan put forward by the twenty–fourth CPSU Party Congress. The article purportedly represented the views of the Soviet population, which were presented to help the American reader interpret the summit. According to the article, the agreement on peaceful coexistence could only mean one thing: "The idea of peaceful coexistence underlying Soviet foreign policy has received worldwide recognition and has become an obvious and significant force of world development." Peaceful coexistence in foreign relations was said to be a Leninist principle that the U.S.S.R. had adhered to since its inception: "This principle continues to be implemented unswervingly" (July 1972:9).

Thus, according to *Soviet Life*, the Moscow Summit disclosed the consistent and principled foreign policy of the Soviet Union, "which has never striven and is not now striving to achieve any advantages at the expense of other countries' interests, but builds its relations with all states on the basis of equality and mutual benefit" (July 1972:9). The U.S.S.R., then, was depicted as the force behind any progress toward better relations between the superpowers. Further, the Soviet Union was portrayed as a peace–loving nation with a fair foreign policy as opposed to the unfair and warlike foreign policy of the United States. Novosti political analyst Spartak Beglov wrote a similar commentary in the January 1973 issue. In addressing the question "Why did it take so long for the principle of peaceful coexistence to be accepted?" Beglov pointed first to the refusal of the Western countries to recognize the socialist countries. Second, he claimed the West believed in the myth that the Soviet Union was exporting revolution; the West was accused of having misused the concept of proletarian internationalism, which is "organically related to socialist ideology." Beglov then implicated the United States as the force opposing peace:

> The principle of peaceful coexistence cannot be extended to the world's social problems, however. There can be no peace between the exploiters and the exploited, between the oppressors and the oppressed. The class struggle goes on and will continue until nothing is left of the remnants of colonialism, neocolonialism and racism, until there is no more imperialist interference in the affairs of nations that have taken the road of social change (January 1973:14).

An abridged article courtesy of *Izvestia* reiterated this theme, contending that:

> The experience of our country shows that a voluntary pooling of the energies and efforts of dozens of nations and nationalities is a powerful counterbalance to the imperialist policy of military gambles, arbitrary rule and cynical toying with the destinies of peoples. (March, 1973:31)

Brezhnev claimed that further progress in Soviet–American relations depended on how the Vietnam War was ended. In his report on the fiftieth anniversary of the U.S.S.R., Brezhnev called the Vietnam War "the longest and dirtiest war in American history," and stated that the Soviet Union wanted to end that war by actively helping "its Vietnamese friends in achieving a just, peaceful settlement." Brezhnev also lashed out at China in his speech, claiming that the Chinese were trying to damage the Soviet Union and the socialist community by making "preposterous claims to Soviet territory," by slandering the Soviet social system, and by sabotaging the disarmament and détente processes (Special Insert, March 1973:II). The Chinese were accused of trying to splinter the socialist and communist movements.

Soviet Life printed a message from the CPSU and the Supreme Soviet "To the Peoples of the World," which followed Brezhnev's speech. The message began as one of "peace, friendship, and brotherhood," in accordance with the principles of "the immortal Lenin." An attack on the United States government followed this introduction: "The disgraceful aggression of the U.S.A. in Vietnam continues. ... The Soviet people, jointly with all peace–loving peoples, wrathfully protest the crimes committed by American imperialism in Vietnam" (Special Insert, March 1973:IV). According to Professor Anatoli Gromyko, the Soviet Union was ready to commit to a peaceful foreign policy, however, "there are still people who cling to the idea of force" (May 1973:14).

Excerpts from Brezhnev's speech at the World Peace Congress, held October 26, 1973, were printed in the January 1974 edition of Soviet Life in an article entitled "For a Just, Democratic Peace, For the Security of Nations and International Cooperation." Brezhnev claimed the principle of noninterference in the internal affairs of other countries was being undermined by "some circles in the West" and was being justified by the "hypocritical slogan of defending human rights in the socialist countries." These people in the West were said to be trying to meddle with the internal order of the socialist countries and/or trying to use détente to weaken those countries. Brezhnev said:

> Let us call a spade a spade, dear friends. They talk of "liberalization," but what they mean is elimination of socialism's real gains and erosion of the sociopolitical rights of the people's of socialist countries ... We have no reason to shun any serious discussion of human rights. Our Revolution, the victory of socialism in this country have not only proclaimed but have secured in reality the rights of the worker of any nationality, the rights of millions of working people, in a way capitalism has been unable to do in any country in the world (January 1974:6).

The problem of human rights was thus discussed in relation to the principle of noninterference in other nations. Spartak Beglov commented on the Forum of Peace Forces and argued that: "Peace is undermined by the expansionist claims of those fond of grabbing others' lands and riches and by the saber rattling of the hawks of the military–industrial complex" (January 1974:8). Finally, the issue printed an appeal from the World Congress of Peace Forces in which a total peace platform was endorsed, and the recent uses of napalm were condemned.

Hail Lenin

Vladimir Ilyich Lenin's thinking is referenced throughout *Soviet Life*, and the magazine often printed excerpts from his speeches and writings. Lenin's words were used to give credibility to articles in *Soviet Life* on nationality issues, literacy, education, health care, conservation and environmental issues, industry, government, Soviet democracy, unemployment, freedom of speech and assembly, the family, women's rights, quality control over consumer goods, the development of Moscow, human development, science, and all aspects of foreign policy. Lenin was thus given credit (or responsibility) for the ideas underlying every aspect of Soviet society.

In addition, Lenin's words were used to legitimize the arguments of many journalists, academicians, and political figures who wrote for *Soviet Life*. The January 1972 issue opened with a chapter from Lenin on "The Essence of Nations," to answer the question "What is a socialist nation?;" the March issue of that year also used Lenin's writings to answer the question "What is Soviet power?" Indeed, Lenin's name appeared in every issue of *Soviet Life*, and his name permeated every aspect of Soviet life. For example, a city in Tajikistan had been named "Leninabad," and a collective farm in the Jewish autonomous region was called "Testament of Lenin."

On the fiftieth anniversary of Lenin's death, an article appeared in the January 1974 issue of *Soviet Life* called "Lenin: Traits of a Genius." The piece emphasized the international significance of Lenin's teaching and work; Lenin was described as an extraordinary man, who gave priority to the common interests of all working people and who never gave in on principles. He was reportedly "profoundly scientific" in his analysis and very democratic in nature. Lenin was said to have been "sparkled with life," and ironically, to have opposed the "cult of the personality" (January 1974:4–5)

In the May 1973 issue, Armand Hammer gave an outline of his experiences in dealing with Lenin, and spoke of Lenin with great respect and admiration. Hammer was the only American authority figure mentioned with any knowledge about Lenin. The November, 1973 issue featured a "Tribute to Lenin" (p. 8) which focused on the Lenin Mausoleum in Red

Square. Lenin was mentioned a total of 269 times in the sample of *Soviet Life* analyzed under Brezhnev. Brezhnev was cited 204 times (see Figure 1).

Figure 1: References to General Secretaries, CPSU, *Soviet Life*, January 1972 to January 1974

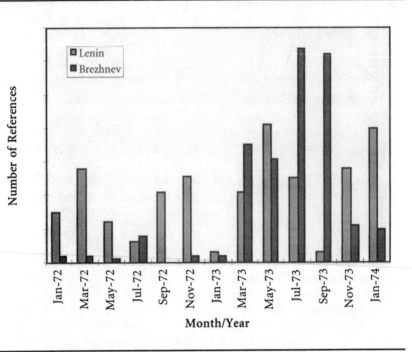

"LETTERS TO THE EDITOR" AND "QUERIES FROM READERS"

To print the letters to the editor of *Soviet Life* would be a superfluous exercise, since they all conveyed basically the same message: one of goodwill and appreciation for the magazine. Almost every letter to the editor was an expression of how much the person enjoyed the magazine. Some of these people said they had traveled in the Soviet Union and found it a wonderful country. One of the letters thanked the editor for continuing to send the magazine even though the school could no longer afford the subscription. Another letter said how lucky the Soviet people were to have had such a dynamic leader as Vladimir Lenin.

Table 1: Topics of "Queries from Readers" *Soviet Life,* **1972–1974**

1	the city Kuibyshev	27	mining of alexandrite
2	employee disagreements with managers	28	antique shops
3	employment in the U.S.S.R.	29	newspapers
4	cultural treatment of death	30	Russian dogs
5	existence of juvenile delinquency	31	U.S.S.R. agriculture
6	Greeks in the Soviet Union	32	the Motherland statue
7	the Moscow Conservatory	33	constituent republics
8	the city Kerch	34	the state language
9	game of checkers	35	medical care costs
10	teenagers earning money	36	Soviet militia tactics
11	private ownership of firearms laws	37	housing construction
12	city of Tomsk	38	inheritance cases
13	the Moscow Conservatory	39	retirement system
14	election of Congresses	40	TV transmission
15	stone figures in the Ukraine and Russia	41	educational system
16	consumer cooperatives	42	Mosfilm agency
17	auto accident injuries	43	medical care
18	life and education in Kazan	44	amateur musicians
19	the cyclist who climbed Mt. Elbrus	45	health resorts
20	publication of books and magazines	46	circuses
21	forest products	47	physical exercises
22	most popular soccer player	48	the city Mogilev
23	cost of playing sports in the U.S.S.R.	49	distribution of goods
24	women in Soviet society	50	psychotropic drug use
25	the song the "internationale"	51	symphony orchestras
26	skiing in the Caucuses	52	the fire brigade

The "Queries from Readers" section, included in each issue of the magazine, was also comprised of friendly questions; at no time did a critical question about the Soviet Union appear. Table 1 lists the topics of questions from American readers which appeared in *Soviet Life.*

While it cannot be proven that these questions were actually from readers, the questions do conveniently reflect those issues the editorial board wanted to address. One question appeared in exactly the same form in two different issues: "It is generally known that Soviet citizens do not have to pay for health care. But how much does it cost the state?" (July 1973:47; November 1973:27). The phrasing of the question suggested that it was written not by American writers but rather by Soviet writers eager to make positive statements about the U.S.S.R.

Some of the questions showed an awkward use of the English language. For example: "How much does it cost to go in for sports in the Soviet Union?" Also the questions addressed topics commonly dealt with in *Soviet Life* feature articles: industry, education, health care, and regions of interest. On a few occasions, the "Queries from Readers" were printed without any references as to whom asked the questions. Generally, a name and city was printed after each question, (for example, Max Miller, Los Angeles, California). If the questions were not contrived by the Novosti staff and were, in fact, real questions from American readers, they clearly were selected for being nonconfrontational.

SUMMARY

The analysis of the Brezhnev era of *Soviet Life* shows a media content and framing that presents an optimal picture of Soviet society. The Soviet "model society" was contrasted with the capitalist societies (particularly the United States), which were afflicted with many problems reflecting an inadequate social system. The Soviet Union was presented as following a fair and moral foreign policy, while the United States was depicted as an imperialist, aggressive nation.

We will now examine the content of *Soviet Life* under Gorbachev, to determine whether the themes change. How would the magazine present Soviet life under Gorbachev?

5

Perestroika and Diplomacy: *Soviet Life* under Gorbachev

As a publication of the Soviet embassy and Novosti Press Agency, we might expect *Soviet Life* to continue to serve its historical role: to put the Soviet Union's best face forward. But how did the Soviet national image presented in *Soviet Life* under Gorbachev differ from that under Brezhnev? In this chapter, we will examine the content of *Soviet Life* under Gorbachev, focusing on 1988 to 1990, at the height of Gorbachev's stability.

VERBAL STYLE

Soviet Life under Gorbachev exhibited the same relatively complex verbal style as during the Brezhnev period. But the magazine was no longer filled with highly technical and scientific articles, although these appeared occasionally. Despite its complex verbal style as compared to the U.S. press, new types of feature columns appeared in *Soviet Life* under Gorbachev that reflected a new style and tone.

For example, a regular column called "How We Live" by Darya Nikolayeva was run in the magazine; this column featured upbeat and amusing aspects of family life as written by a wife and mother. The column can be best compared to the work of Erma Bombeck in the American press except that the themes of perestroika and glasnost were woven into Nikolayeva's stories.

Soviet Life continued running reprinted articles from other Soviet publications, although these included not only official newspapers such as *Pravda* and *Izvestia*, but also periodicals born of glasnost policies, such as the radical magazine *Ogonyok*. The reprints gleaned information about the Soviet press' overall development, and highlighted the continued interrelationships among the various publications.

THE MAGAZINE'S AUDIENCE

Because the content of *Soviet Life* during this period stressed the social, historical, economic, and political problems of Soviet society, the publication seemed to be intended for a relatively sophisticated audience; that is, people who knew something about Soviet history and politics, and who were generally concerned about developments in the Soviet Union. Under Brezhnev, issues of *Soviet Life* contained numerous scientific, academic, and political articles with a content geared toward several specialized audiences. The magazine now assumed some prior knowledge by the reader, yet its content was more accessible to the non specialist than during the Brezhnev period.

THE MAGAZINE'S COVERAGE

One of the most striking differences between *Soviet Life* from 1988 to 1990 as compared to 1972 to 1974 is the absence of a stock group of journalists writing for the magazine. Instead, political commentary was written by various journalists and scholars. Scholars continued writing many of the articles on various scientific, theoretical, and social issues. Other articles were often written by journalists from other newspapers and magazines. The only consistently featured writer was Darya Nikolayeva.

Soviet Life now referenced American media at times, including *Time* magazine's Moscow bureau chief John Kohan about his view of the changes occurring in the Soviet Union (July 1989); *Newsweek's* coverage of better relations between the U.S. and U.S.S.R. (March 1989); CNN's story on the nineteenth Party Conference (September 1988); PBS's documentary on the U.S.S.R. (May 1989); *The New York Times'* coverage of the impact for the Communist Party of the elections for the Congress of People's Deputies (May 1989); and *Foreign Affairs'* format, as a model for the Soviet political monthly *Mezhdunarodnaya Zhizn* (International Affairs) (January 1989).

THE MAGAZINE'S CAST

The cast of *Soviet Life* under Gorbachev fell into two broad categories: people representing the perversion of socialism, the resultant stagnation of Soviet society, and resistance to change; and people representing progress and change consistent with perestroika and glasnost. These categories can be crudely seen as representing the bad and good citizens. Within each of these two categories, a primary and secondary cast were developed.

CORRUPTION, STAGNATION, AND RESISTANCE

The Primary Cast

The primary cast in this category included two authority figures who corrupted their power, resulting in misguided socialism. The main figure in this cast was Joseph Stalin, who was absent from earlier issues analyzed, but was resurrected in May 1988 and remained in the issues through 1990. The second authority figure in this category was Leonid Brezhnev, whose tenure was repeatedly labeled as "the years of stagnation." Brezhnev was not mentioned in *Soviet Life* until January 1989, after which he was referenced in all but two issues (July and November 1989).

The Secondary Cast

The secondary cast included contemporary Soviet officials, middle managers, bureaucrats, and workers who resisted Gorbachev's policies of openness, democratization, and restructuring. Most often, these figures were not named specifically, but rather alluded to, for example, "we have begun to get rid of excessive politeness and humbleness in the presence of a VIP who is unable to answer any question but can expertly beat around the bush for hours" (May 1988:9). These people were depicted as either unwilling to change, as they would have to relinquish their privileges, or as "dead weight"—too lazy to change. They served as the antitheses of the "model perestroishchik" discussed below.

PROGRESS AND CHANGE: THE CAST

The Primary Cast

The cast for "progress and change" included authority figures who framed the publication's content based on their access to power—either political or intellectual. The first member of this group was the magazine editor. At the beginning of this period, the editor–in–chief was Vladimir V. Belyakov, the Washington editor was Oleg P. Benyukh, and the managing editor was Victor L. Karasin. In May 1988 Robert Tsfasman, a Novosti reporter under Brezhnev, became editor–in–chief. The editorial shift was not accompanied by a significant change in the magazine's content; both Belyakov and Tsfasman served essentially the same function as earlier editors: They set the stage for the remaining contents of the issue and outlined various Soviet policy positions. But the content of their columns was markedly different from that of earlier editors. Both of these editors signed their names under the "Editor's Notes" section, in contrast to Alexander Makarov, who was editor–in–chief of *Soviet Life* under Brezhnev.

The progress and change primary cast also relied on the two most prominent authority figures: Vladimir Lenin and Mikhail Gorbachev. They appeared more than any others, with Lenin referenced in all but three issues of *Soviet Life* during this period (November 1988; July 1989, and January 1990); Gorbachev appeared in every issue (see Figure 2).

Figure 2: References to General Secretaries, CPSU, *Soviet Life*, January 1988 to January 1990

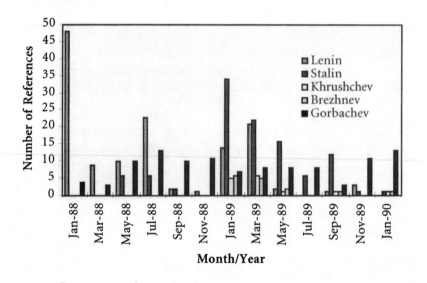

The third category of authority figures in the primary cast were officials and academicians who supported Gorbachev's programs. They wrote articles for *Soviet Life* that stressed the urgent need for reform and restructuring and espoused the values of greater openness and the democratization of society. They also served to delegitimate past policies, denouncing the crimes of Stalin and Brezhnev, filling in the historical gaps, and setting current policies in accordance with "true" Leninism.

The fourth group of authority figures in the primary cast were journalists, artists, musicians, and playwrights, who as the representatives of cultural production, could describe the oppression of the past and advocate greater freedom for the present. Interestingly, some of these journalists played prominent roles in both the Brezhnev and Gorbachev eras, including

Gennadi Gerasimov (Novosti journalist) and Vladimir Pozner (Novosti journalist and television commentator). The artists, however, were presented as dissidents who were censored under Brezhnev, but celebrated under Gorbachev.

The final group of authority figures in the primary cast were prominent Americans who promoted a market economy and democratic political processes in the Soviet Union; some of them served as consultants to the process, such as prominent businesspersons Harold Willens and Wesley Bilsen of California.

The Secondary Cast

The secondary cast advocated and legitimated the discourse of the primary cast. The secondary cast included two types of figures: the "model perestroishchik;" and the victims of past policies.

The most covered model perestroishchik was the plant or farm manager who applied the principles of cost efficiency, consistent with perestroika. Despite resistance from those who were lazy or hesitant to give up their old ways, the efficient manager persevered to modernize Soviet production. These workers were shown to be willing to sacrifice in the short term in order to change the Soviet economic system in the long run. For example, Buri Karimov, a young engineer who turned an ailing road–building firm profitable was heralded in an article called "A Self–Made Man" (January 1989:20).

The second type of model perestroishchik was the entrepreneur who had the drive and initiative to begin a new business. Often this category included those with newly formed joint ventures with American businesspersons.

The victims of the past showed that Stalin's and Brezhnev's policies had failed miserably resulting in a series of social problems affecting particular groups of people. In a broad sense, everyone in Soviet society had been victimized, since the prevailing economic system worked so inefficiently and the political system so undemocratically. Crime was shown as a serious social problem on the rise, with a strong element of organized crime that threatened everyone's safety and corrupted the Soviet economy. Several groups received special attention as victims of the past. The preoccupation of *Soviet Life* with youth continued, but it presented a very different picture of young people from that of the 1970s. Now they were shown to be alienated from society, disenchanted with hopes for change, and suffering the ravages of drug abuse and delinquency.

Women were shown as having been betrayed by past policies, which promised them equality with men but only increased their workload and maintained discrimination. Thus, while past issues of *Soviet Life* used women who expounded the virtues of socialism in promoting equality for women and men in Soviet society, more recent issues depicted women as victims of the system.

The final group of victims included workers, or average citizens. The Soviet worker, rather than serving the state dutifully and efficiently as depicted previously, was now shown as incapable of independent thinking due to having been so heavily managed over the years. This group of victims was presented as a possible threat to Gorbachev's policies, since perestroika relied on enterprising not lazy people.

THE MAGAZINE'S SETTINGS

While *Soviet Life* continued its focus on a geographical area in each issue, the magazine's content did not center on that region as in the past. Nevertheless, the magazine would sometimes carry several articles on a region to show the operation of perestroika there.

MEDIA FRAMES

The content of *Soviet Life* under Gorbachev no longer presented the overwhelmingly positive image of the Soviet Union for readers. Instead, the magazine dealt with many problems in Soviet life, their roots in history, and the efforts to resolve them. The content was organized around seven frames, including: 1. the continuing revolution, 2. catharsis, 3. the years of stagnation, 4. rampant social problems, 5. rescue, 6. glasnost, and 7. the new culture frame.

The Continuing Revolution

Soviet Life presented Gorbachev's policies of openness, restructuring, and democratization as a return to the mission of the October 1917 Revolution and to Vladimir Lenin's policies. The January 1988 issue pictured the hammer and sickle insignia over the number 70 (representing seventy years) with Red Square beneath them. The cover heading stated "The Revolution Continues." In an article entitled "Humanity's Finest Hour: The 70th Anniversary of the October Revolution," Pavel Antonov concluded that the socialist choice made in 1917 was correct, and that "we progress only when we are seeking a higher form of social organization, socialism. This fundamental conclusion made by Lenin is as valid today as it was in his day" (January 1988:3). He claimed that perestroika would ensure the Soviet Union's ascent and create conditions for peaceful coexistence.

The principle of peaceful coexistence was shown to be grounded in Lenin's thought as well, so that Gorbachev's plans for reducing tensions between the superpowers was shown to be a natural extension of Lenin's policies. Valentin Falin, the board chairman of APN, stated in a published discussion with *Izvestia* political analyst Alexander Bovin, "To Lenin belongs the formula: There may arise a situation where class interests will have to be sacrificed in the name of broader interests." The discussants went on to note the October Revolution's major contributions to civilization; namely, the principle of peaceful coexistence and the possibility of building "a world of equal nations in which all processes are directed democratically" (January 1988:40).

The March 1988 issue printed an abridged version of Gorbachev's speech at a meeting of top mass media executives, scholarly institutions, and creative workers delivered at CPSU Headquarters. The speech, entitled "Democratization—the Essence of Perestroika, the Essence of Socialism," depicted perestroika as a continuation of the revolution, since the Soviet Union was said to be "at the threshold of a second stage of restructuring." Gorbachev also noted that "we subscribe to Lenin's concept of political party, which should be the vanguard of society." (March 1988:1) Lenin was invoked to justify the Communist Party's continuing role, which was necessary but "must not lag behind the processes taking place in society" (March 1988:12).

During his meeting with the Patriarch Pimen and Holy Synod members, Gorbachev described the new principle of church freedom as that of rectifying socialist principles that were cast aside under Stalin. He stated, "We are restoring now in full measure the Leninist principles of attitudes toward religion, Church, and believers" (July 1988:39).

Movement toward a more democratic style of decisionmaking and elections was also grounded in Lenin's thought. Novosti political analyst Mikhail Poltoranin, who analyzed a Gorbachev speech at the nineteenth Party Conference, noted that he called for "a complete restoration of Lenin's principle of collective discussion and decision making" (September 1988:35). The delegates decided that the number of candidates for seats should exceed the number to be filled.

Agrarian reforms implemented by Gorbachev were described as consistent with Lenin's New Economic Policy (NEP), in an "effort to bring innovation and rejuvenation to the grossly neglected and stagnant economy of the Soviet village" (March 1989:4). In a reprint from *Ogonyok* by historian Vladimir Glotov, perestroika was described as "a revolution from above, in the tradition of Russian history, in which movement from the top to bottom is prevalent" (March 1989:54). Roy Medvedev, a prominent Soviet historian and Gorbachev supporter, summarized the message of the continuing revolution frame in the final words of his essay "What Society Are We

Rebuilding?" by exclaiming, "We want the ideals and tasks of the October 1917 Revolution implemented in full measure" (January 1989:13).

Catharsis

Much of the content of *Soviet Life* expressed outrage at the policies carried out by Joseph Stalin. Historical essays often set out to fill in gaps regarding Stalin's activities. For example, a historical piece on party conferences, reprinted from *Pravda* by the historian Vasil Bondar, suggested that Lenin's cooperative movement was working until "unfortunately, later on, when administration by injunction kept developing and democracy kept receding, the very idea of the cooperative movement was defied, its role depreciated and its multiformity lost." The article then describes Stalin's violations of democratic inner–party leadership and authoritarian style, indicating that the party did not have a single conference or congress between 1941 and 1952. The author continues:

> Stalin's boundless arrogance and disdain for the opinion of others were not the whole point, to my mind, he might have been afraid of being exposed in his lifetime, and a party assembly could become a place for that. After all, the Soviet victory in the 1941–45 Great Patriotic War against Nazi Germany had helped many people to get rid of their psychology of "small cogs" in the government machine, which had been imposed on them from above. Maybe that caused another wave of repressions after the war, with the same, familiar way of doing away with the "obstinate." (July 1988:9)

Eduardas Juhnevicius, a Lithuanian poet and artist interviewed by *Soviet Life*, was asked if Stalin was his political idol, since the interviewer found Stalin's picture in the artist's workshop. Juhnevicius responded that, to the contrary, Stalin was "the antipode. Each time I look at the photo, I try to fathom the full measure of his treachery and cruelty. For me, he is the epitome of evil, while I try to make the world kinder." Juhnevicius was described by *Soviet Life* as "a lover of truth and an ardent supporter of perestroika, which has touched all spheres of life" (September 1988:62).

The cathartic frame included not only a villification of Stalin, but also a reinterpretation of history which rehabilitated Stalin's rivals—Nikolai Bukharin, Leon Trotsky, and Grigori Zinoviev, and which treated Khrushchev as a well–intentioned, albeit incompetent leader. Roy Medvedev reproached Stalin in his interpretation of history:

Along with people who sincerely wished to build a better society, there were some, like Stalin, who strove for personal power. And such people were developing an authoritarian, totalitarian system in socialist disguise. Leaders like Khrushchev were devoted to socialism and to the people. But because they had no idea about the methods of socialist construction, their good intentions resulted only in distorted political, economic and ideological forms ... In the late 1920s there were alternative forces to the command–style system of administration that Stalin had created. Nikolai Bukharin, for one, represented such alternative forces. He supported Lenin's New Economic Policy, broader development of various forms of cooperation and democratic principles. But Stalin managed to gain the upper hand ... the people who were imprisoned under Stalin were slaves by all social standards. (January 1989:13)

This excerpt from a January 1989 article entitled "Stalin is My Idol!" referred to an unnamed individual who defended and worshiped Stalin; the article indicts him in the most vitriolic fashion. This piece also offered a different view from Medvedev's toward Khrushchev—Khrushchev and Brezhnev were both presented as continuations of Stalinism:

The vast majority of deviations from socialism, many of which have not yet been overcome, emerged in Stalin's time. Khrushchev's and Brezhnev's flaws and errors were also recurrences of Stalinism. Stalinism means not just the personality cult, an innocent belief in god–man. It means usurpation of power over the party and the people, disguised by the distortion of Lenin's ideas, of revolution and socialism. It means deformation of the party. Stalinism implies mass terror, contempt for human life, the massacre of millions of innocent people on political grounds. It is the system of administration by decree embracing all spheres of social life, formed by the rule and subject to him only; enormous powers wielded by bureaucrats; corruption in management; trade, science, and so forth. Stalinism is a blatant violation of the simplest democratic norms, artfully muted by rhetoric about human rights; absence of a law–based state; unchecked intolerance of heterodoxy; distortions of Lenin's nationalities policy; and arbitrary treatment of religion.

Stalinism means forced labor of millions of people, primitive technology, plundering of human and natural resources. It is sponging and social inequality generated by leveling on the one hand, and privileges to certain strata of the population on the other. Stalinism implies mistrust, suspicion, denunciation, obsequiousness, hypocrisy, erosion of human dignity. Stalinism means fraud on the state level, fabrication of "traitors against the homeland," misrepresented results of collectivization, falsified history of the party, the state, and the world.

Stalinism is a militant obscurantism, persecution of intellectuals; it is the great "luminary of science" interfering in many fields, after which they ceased to exist for many years. To the honor of the party and the people, not everyone was submissive to the spiritual and other pressures of Stalinism and its varieties. Stalinism failed to erase people's intelligence, integrity and honesty. Revolutionary perestroika, the decisions of the Twenty– seventh Congress of the CPSU and the Nineteenth Party Conference, revive Leninism ... Weeds should be removed roots and all. That is why the press focuses today on the deep roots of our troubles. (January 1989:25)

Yuri Afanasyev, a prominent Soviet historian, argued that the incriminations of Stalin were necessary "to revive the social consciousness of the community in order to cast off the evil spell of Stalinism." A party member named Zhanna Zinchenko asked if "Stalin and his gang are still members of our Communist Party. Can we tolerate this?" She called for posthumously expelling Stalin and his lackeys from the party, and asked: "When will we hear that they have been judged? When will we remove their graves from Red Square?" (May, 1989:25–26).

The Years of Stagnation

This frame organized material about the Brezhnev era, commonly described as the "years of stagnation," during which many problems initiated by Stalin went uncorrected, new social problems were created, and the massive Soviet bureaucracy solidified its stronghold.

The town of Gus Khrustalny served as a case study on the effects of Brezhnev's reign. According to a feature article in the January 1989 issue, bureaucrats spoiled the town's charm by erecting drab, faceless, Soviet housing that looked the same in all Soviet towns. Laborers, betrayed by the constitutional concept of ownership of the means of production by the people, were alienated from their work.

According to economist Gennadi Lisichkin, the years of stagnation exacted a terrible cost on society. The people had become so spoiled by years of freeloading off the system that they would not accept perestroika, which demanded hard work and efficiency (January 1988). In addition, the years of stagnation were marked by misinformation and propaganda, which compounded people's indifference with feelings of betrayal.

The model perestroishchik confronted the years of stagnation by either attempting to reform the system, or by taking on a more challenging, individualistic job. One woman forest manager went to work in the Carpathian Mountains. She claimed, "I left because I was sick of the empty talk, the hypocrisy, the high–sounding words." *Soviet Life* also noted: "Once a 'yessing' honor student and a disenchanted loner, Mashina is becoming an energetic leader with high principles, who is fighting for the life of the Carpathian Mountains" (January 1988:25–26). Another model perestroishchik, referred to as Ivar, turned to drugs after adults lied to him about the Komsomol. Ivar moved to the country and started a farm to seek out some "freedom from bureaucracy, red tape, and hypocrisy." *Soviet Life* commented that "Years of boasting and hypocritical reportage of more and more victories in all walks of life had led our country's young people to feel cynical and indifferent, and to just want to get away from all the hype" (November 1989:22).

The Brezhnev years were described as blatantly undemocratic in an article reprinted from *Pravda* that claimed:

> "legal nihilism" ... and public ignorance of the law created
> the framework for flagrant violations of law in the Brezhnev
> era. The incompetence or outright dishonesty of officials
> was compounded by imperfections in the legal system.
> (July, 1988:6)

Editor Robert Tsfasman admitted in his "Editor's Notes" section that he looked at an old issue of *Soviet Life* in which a trade union leader said there were no strikes in the Soviet Union because any disagreements were settled peacefully. Tsfasman said he could not blame the man for saying what he was supposed to say, but claimed *The Washington Post* was right in suggesting, about miner's strikes, that "only a couple of years ago the Kremlin would have taken the worker's massive manifestations as an inadmissible affront to its authority" (September 1989:1).

Artists were also censored under Brezhnev. In an interview, artist Vyacheslav Kalinin noted:

The officials were always pretty harsh to artists they didn't
like. In the early seventies they came down on us especially
hard. A lot of authors, artists, and musicians had to
emigrate. But there were quite a few of us who thought our
inspiration would dry up if we left and that the commercial
success we could get in the West would tempt us to
compromise our art. So we just kept going. (May 1989:61)

Soviet Life called for Brezhnev's remains to be removed from the
Lenin mausoleum, and for measures to be taken to remove his name from
any honorable position in the historical record. Yet one article noted that
while "the awarding of the highest prize for literature to Brezhnev is a
shameful, yet typical fact of our recent past ... what would we change today
by cancelling this decision? ... As one poet stated, what's done is done"
(January 1989:28).

Rampant Social Problems

In marked contrast to earlier issues, Soviet Life under Gorbachev
frankly admitted the nation's many social problems. In earlier issues, human
rights issues were framed within the Soviet definition, which showed that the
Soviet system provided for its citizens more extensively than any other
nation. Under Gorbachev, the question of human rights took on new
meaning, with individual freedom as a major component: freedom of
religion, information, emigration, and so forth. Mikhail Poltoranin, a
political analyst for Novosti, noted:

What surprised me most about the conference was a long
and detailed passage about human rights in Mikhail
Gorbachev's speech. I may be told that this topic was always
present in the speeches of Soviet leaders; it was, but it was
taken up with the express purpose of reproaching the West,
of piling up allegations around a nonexistent problem, and
of proclaiming that we were impeccable in this sphere.
(September 1988:9)

Gorbachev argued that the church had played a major role in
Russian history and culture and noted that the separation of church and state
would make sure that "no one can interfere in believers' affairs: Freedom of
religion is guaranteed by the constitution" (July 1988:40). Still, an engineer
claimed he was discriminated against at his job due to his religious beliefs
(July 1988). Soviet Life reported that local government officials often ignore

complaints levied by believers, but that perestroika sought to eliminate these practices (July 1988).

Housing was also shown by *Soviet Life* to be in short supply. Those available were accused of being drab and of poor quality. Air and water quality were shown to be declining as well. Youth symbolized the problems in Soviet society, and these were discussed candidly in *Soviet Life*. In an article called "Is it Easy to be Young?" Kestutis Oginskas detailed the new, more realistic assessment of Soviet youth:

> Until recently we thought youth was synonymous with everything bright and carefree. We were so utterly convinced that our young people were all "clean and good" and traditionally loyal to the ideals of their fathers that we began to indulge in wishful thinking. But gradually reality started pushing our illusions into the background, and we began to notice symptoms of a grave, long–neglected malaise. We ... resorted to time–worn slogans and appeals that we adults really did not believe in. (September 1988:49)

Noting that the number of young people joining the Komsomol was down, Oginskas argued that most of them had little, if any, confidence in the corrupt and bureaucratized institution. Children with little else to do were reportedly turning to delinquency and drugs. Drug and alcohol addiction were acknowledged Soviet social problems too. The emphasis on punishment as a method of deterrence was shown to be shifting to a medical model of substance abuse, with solutions concentrating on education, prevention, and recovery (November 1988). The U.S. group Alcoholics Anonymous introduced its recovery program in several Soviet cities.

Crime was also shown to be an escalating problem in the Soviet Union. A piece that focused on the Soviet mafia noted that "contrary to what was thought, Soviet society is not immune to organized crime" (March 1989:45). According to the feature, the mafia began to appear under Khrushchev and had since grown to control much of the black market.

In her commentaries on being a wife, mother, and grandmother, Darya Nikolayeva argued that women face "double duty" and economic problems caused by shortages in consumer goods, such as for baby items (November 1988:53). Family and health problems were raised in another article; in particular, the shortage of contraceptives in the Soviet Union was linked to the high number of abortions (March 1989:10).

In 1989, *Soviet Life* presented the status of women very differently from that of the 1970 status. According to a commentary by Vitalina Koval:

Many thought the "women's problem" did not exist in the
Soviet Union. How could it? After all, women were granted
equal rights with men soon after the Revolution. But now
problems that Soviet women have been facing all along are
coming to light. (March 1989:24)

Women with a specialized secondary education were reported to
comprise sixty–one percent of all workers; nonetheless, they occupied those
jobs "on a lower rung of the career ladder than their male counterparts"
(March 1989:24), and earned thirty percent less income. As in the United
States, the problems of the decline of the nuclear family, of single–female
parenting, and of "latchkey children" were noted. The pervasive sexism
within Soviet society was evidenced by a *Soviet Life* article on female music
star Laima Vaikula, in which she was described as "something of a
workaholic, she has much in common with her 'career woman' ... But unlike
the career woman, Vaikula remains every inch a charming woman"
(November 1988:40).

An article reprinted from *Literaturnaya Gazeta* by Zoya
Boguslavskaya claimed that destructive processes were occurring in the lives
of Soviet women, and that "no one has calculated the price we women have
to pay for the right to act like men" (March 1988:16). The news produced
during the Gorbachev era regarding the status of Soviet women had changed
markedly from that produced during the Brezhnev era.

Another social problem that was acknowledged was the inability of
Soviet society to provide sufficient consumer products. Soviet legislation, red
tape, and difficult economic conditions were said to discourage investors and
the success of joint–ventures. In a radical article entitled "Good–Bye Mr.
President: Reflections on Ronald Reagan's Presidency," *Izvestia* political
observer Stanislav Kondrashov suggested:

I think there must be 20 times as many private cars and a
thousand times as many PCs in the United States as in the
Soviet Union. For a long time we lived in a world of make–
believe, pretending that this was better for the health of the
nation than facing up to the "ugly truth." Now we have
changed our attitude—we are more open about our own
shortcomings, and that makes us less willing to point out
the failings of others. True, capitalist society is far from
perfect, but two wrongs don't make a right. The more we
were drawn into self–deception, the more painful it was to
come back to reality. And when we finally took off our
blinders, we saw that industrialized capitalist states, which
were not afraid to face the "ugly truth," had coped far better

than we had with some of the challenges that the October Revolution had posed before humankind: providing the people with social and medical protection, an education, a decent wage and a reasonable pension in old age. (March 1989:38)

Rescue

Perestroika, demokratizatsiya, and glasnost, according to *Soviet Life*, held the potential to rescue Soviet society from its web of problems. Already there were several areas of progress. *Soviet Life* carried a section in the magazine called "Perestroika in Action," in which such progress was detailed. At the nineteenth Party Conference, Gorbachev asked delegates to be ardent partisans of perestroika, since "bureaucrats are fighting tooth and nail for the remnants of the stagnation system, which allowed incompetent bunglers to rise to major positions" (July 1988:4).

Workers at the Taurus television plant reported that perestroika was moving very slowly there, so that the plant still took orders from above. The result was that "having no rights is bad for both product quality and personnel morale," and thus workers and managers were "ready to throw all their weight behind perestroika" (September 1988:28).

According to *Soviet Life*, the effects of perestroika, democratization, and glasnost were already evident at the plant, as supervisors were elected, to guard "against bureaucracy and incompetence." One worker noted: "Another thing is that we don't need to keep a lot of extra people on the team. We can get rid of the deadwood" (September 1988:28). An article on a professional engineer's club noted the change in the engineer's role with the advent of perestroika:

> Even those who have become accustomed to a "quiet and peaceful life" have had to work harder under the new economic conditions—that is, under a system of profit–and–loss accounting and self–financing. At the same time better opportunities exist for people who have innovative ideas and approaches. (September 1988:38)

When the Lithuanian city of Siauliai faced the crisis of alienated youth in which "hundreds of Siauliai boys and girls did not know what to do with themselves in the evenings," *Soviet Life* stated that "the need for more radical changes was in the air, and perestroika came in time to make them a reality" (September 1988:49–50). The children were enlisted to help renovate the city. It was stated that "Perestroika has allowed the young to speak out openly on issues that concern them ... They have become active and demand to have their say on issues and problems that previously were decided only by the few" (March 1989:35).

Solving the problems of the elderly and of women also called for perestroika. In the commentary by Vitalina Koval which explained women's problems, the author claimed that:

> Under perestroika, where people and their interests are the goal of all reforms, Soviet society is striving to provide a more comfortable life for its senior citizens, male and female alike ... An honest appraisal of women's problems and realistic plans for solving them make us feel optimistic that major improvements are in the offing. (March 1989:25)

Perestroika was also beckoned to reverse the destruction of the natural environment. In an interview, the chair of the State Committee on Conservation argued that cost accounting and self–financing were essential components of a solution; "perestroika and glasnost are a must" (November 1988:16).

One *Soviet Life* feature described several cases of ill people for whom none of the conventional treatments had worked. But perestroika had allowed alternative medical practitioners to develop new techniques. These doctors were described as heroes "whose new methods of treatment ... have managed to render medical aid to those for whom the generally accepted methods of treatment failed to do anything." The article also claimed that "perestroika is designed particularly for such people, and not for those who for years stood in the way of unusual methods and progress" (November 1988:52).

Although little progress had been made in this area, perestroika promised to rescue the country from its shortage of consumer goods. Boris Alexeyev noted that consumer goods production, under Gorbachev's policy of perestroika, was for the first time a greater economic priority than the means of production (January 1990:39).

Democratization and glasnost offered the nation the opportunity to escape its patterns of propaganda and censorship. According to editor Robert Tsfasman, Pushkin Square had become Moscow's "Hyde Park," where people gathered to debate social and political issues without fear of repercussions. Foreign correspondents were free to go there and observe, since "the days of spy mania are gone" (May 1989:1). *Soviet Life* noted that only five per cent of Muscovites were unwilling to participate anonymously in a recent public opinion poll, and that ninety–three percent of respondents favored perestroika. The study indicated that only eight percent of those surveyed knew what an opinion poll was, and that eighty–eight percent of them wanted to participate in more of them (May 1989:6–7).

Glasnost

Perhaps the greatest achievements under Gorbachev occurred under his policy of glasnost, or openness. *Soviet Life* devoted a section of the magazine to displaying evidence of greater press freedom; the section was titled "Glasnost: Reprints From the Soviet Press" or "Glasnost: The Soviet Press at Work." Excerpts from various Soviet publications were reprinted to show the diversity of opinions expressed and the bold, investigative reporting which characterized the new era. Additionally, *Soviet Life* often had feature articles that dealt with glasnost in many areas of life and media. While there was a broad range of opinions and bold news accounts in comparison to those produced during the Brezhnev years, there nonetheless was a great deal of effort spent on showing the reader how open the press was. Glasnost in *Soviet Life* was conspicuous.

In the January 1988 issue, Editor Belyakov said in his "Editor's Notes" section that he had received an angry letter from an American who had canceled his subscription because the magazine did not feature a "letters to the editor" section or questions from readers. Belyakov stated that he had received many such letters, and therefore was reinstating the sections that they had featured in the past. He wrote:

> True, at that time letters for the section, usually picked from the fan mail, often began with such words: "I'm fond of your magazine," or "*Soviet Life* is one of the most popular publications in the United States." Letters from the negative mail ("I don't like the magazine") containing the word "propaganda" and the like, were put aside more often than not ... Now we shall publish in the "Letters to the Editor" section a wide range of views and different proposals. (March 1988:1)

Indeed, the "Letters to the Editor" section of that issue and later ones included a mixture of critical and complimentary letters. One notable letter came from Elizabeth Richter of Sacramento, California:

> Your magazine is excellent in terms of photography, articles on art and dance and folk crafts. But I learn very little about the Soviet Union in general. The magazine is so full of prevarications and propagandizing that I can't get a clear picture of Soviet society. Thus, it doesn't really seem worth the time reading it. You can get back in touch with me when you can stop making outrageously false statements like there is no illiteracy or unemployment and there are no

homeless people in your country. I wish for the sake of your country that these statements were true, but you and I both know they aren't. Because they aren't about any country in the world. (March 1988:1)

Another letter questioned the sincerity of glasnost and democratization:

The July issue on Christianity in the U.S.S.R. is disappointing in view of the enlightenment of glasnost. There is no way one can describe 1,000 years of Christianity in the U.S.S.R. and Russia, or "Russian Christianity" as you term it, without revealing that there were some 75,000 churches before the Revolution, and possibly 7,000 now. You mention 19 monasteries but there were probably 1,000 at that time. The clergy of the present church are, in fact, government employees, and their education, ordination, and appointment to higher positions in the church are tightly controlled and supervised. Religious education without government sanction, outside the home, I believe, is a criminal offense. These are but a few differences between a state–controlled (Ministry of Religion) church and the free churches of a democratic country. Please, in the spirit of glasnost stop treating your American readers as if we've lived in darkness for the past 70 years. We appreciate the changes that are taking place in the U.S.S.R., but we experienced the birth of freedom some 200 years ago and are still struggling to overcome the obstacles of human nature, color, creed, ethnocentrism, etc. Just saying "glasnost" and "perestroika" doesn't create any magical cures after 70 years of repression and secretive government, but a bit more truth and a little less propaganda will certainly help to convince some of us that these glowing and hopeful slogans may be for real. (November 1988:1)

Two other letters that complimented the magazine and the new Soviet policies were also printed. Criticism of Soviet society extended to many fronts. Even then U.S. Defense Secretary Frank Carlucci was quoted as saying that there was still mistrust in his country of the Soviet government since it refused to release reliable information about its military budget and retained an offensive military posture. The article hinted that according to Soviet colleagues, full disclosure of the budget would occur soon (November 1988). In a later issue, Soviet Foreign Minister Eduard Shevardnadze remarked that military departments and the defense industry, which were formerly immune to criticism, were being put under the control of elective bodies and defense budgets would be made public (January 1989).

The press was depicted as at the forefront of the struggle for democratization. Even the Siauliai local newspaper, while "not as popular as the newspapers of Moscow and Vilnius which, in our present time of openness have so much to say to the reader; nevertheless, by midday is completely sold out" (September 1988:45). While the newspaper represented the city party committee and the city Soviet of People's Deputies, it was described as having "a reputation for being a staunch fighter against bureaucracy at all levels, against verbiage, mismanagement and violations of human rights" (September 1988:45).

Soviet Life indicated that the political monthly *Mezhdunarodnaya Zhizn* (International Affairs), which had been "the most dogmatic of all Soviet publications" (September 1988:11), was changing to resemble, and compete with, the American journal *Foreign Affairs*. The Soviet monthly had begun to feature foreign, especially Western viewpoints, in its spectrum of opinions, including recent contributions from then Secretary of State George Schultz and President Ronald Reagan.

Reprints from the Soviet press offered the chance to see that other Soviet publications were also expressing a greater diversity of opinions. For example, *Izvestia* scolded state statisticians for their past attempts to disguise the consumer market situation in the nation (March 1989). Another *Izvestia* reprint compared the problems of the United States and the Soviet Union, arguing that in both countries, budget deficits were rooted in massive military spending and that paradoxically both nations were now steeped in a bureaucracy that must be dismantled to allow a return to democracy (March 1989). Student newspapers in the U.S.S.R. and the United States were reported as having developed a "newspaper bridge," in which they exchanged information directly, a credit to glasnost. Interestingly, Novosti had taken on the task of organizing the exchanges, and printed an offer to be the mediator and translator of articles for more of these exchanges. *Soviet Life* printed an address at Novosti Press Agency to which people could write (January 1989).

Robert Tsfasman quoted Gorbachev in a later "Editor's Notes" section, stating that "the entire country has become one big debating club" (July 1988:1). Progress was shown in the dramatic changes to Soviet television, which was no longer heavily censored. The May 1988 issue focused on Soviet television and its new programs. One talk show called "The 12th Floor" featured young people who were allowed to question officials about social and political problems.

While the technology had been available since the 1960s, *Soviet Life* argued that telephone call–in programs and teleconferences via satellite were the result of glasnost (May 1988). *Soviet Life* published the transcripts of a televised debate on human rights between representatives of the White House and the Kremlin. The debate, hosted by Peter Jennings of ABC and Leonid Zolotarevsky of Gosteleradio, featured heated arguments about the prevailing definitions of human rights and alleged violations of them.

Soviet Life included the results of a poll of Soviet viewers that revealed that the American panelists were seen as more active, easy–going, and skillful in their discussions (May 1988). Television was portrayed as being able to stimulate political ideas and to accelerate the public consciousness. It was described as the "result, condition, and guarantee of democratization" (May 1988:9). The television political commentator Lev Voznesensky explained in an interview how he had been sent to a camp for political prisoners during the Stalinist purges. On his show, officials have to respond to the public while on the air. Voznesensky claimed that he finally got the program on the air in 1980 after a long, difficult battle:

> Certainly, it was limited to science. Certainly, the program's panel comprised the "well–meaning" president of the Academy of Sciences and four of its vice presidents. Certainly, the public had only five telephone lines on which to call in questions. But the program was a crucial victory.

The program then expanded to 90 minutes and to 20 phone lines (May 1988).

Still, Soviet Life exposed existing bans on openness. Izvestia political correspondent Maxim Yusin posed several questions to Deputy Foreign Minister Vladimir Petrovsky that were reprinted in the magazine. Yusin asked why the Soviet people were not allowed to watch Western television, why Western newspapers and magazines were available only in special reading rooms in libraries, and why xerox machines were still under strict control. Petrovsky responded that the U.S.S.R. would "conform to European standards and truly embrace glasnost." He claimed that all restrictions would be lifted, and that only propaganda on war, racism, pornography, and calls to overthrow the existing regime were forbidden. Petrovsky could not say how long these changes would take to implement fully, as there was some trouble with "the old mentality" (January 1990:12).

New Culture

The content of Soviet Life indicated that new cultural forms were being integrated into Soviet society; some of these consisted simply of old forms reemerging, but many of these were ideas recently adopted from the West.

Artistic and religious culture, while not entirely new, took on forms that were previously prohibited by the state. For example, youth theater was said to be more democratic and to involve more amateur studios. In addition, the Ministry of Culture stopped setting the theme for youth festivals (March 1988). Avant–garde art produced between 1905 and 1930, which had been forced underground by the authorities, was reported as now being acceptable and was to be shown at an exhibit entitled "Time of Change" (January 1989). Other artists who were suppressed under Stalin, Khrushchev, and Brezhnev because their work "stood in contrast to the 'anti–painting' of socialist realism," were finally allowed recognition (January 1990:50).

Moscow was also reported to be experiencing a rock music explosion. A concert held in Moscow was compared to the United States' Woodstock, except that it was not associated with drugs. In fact, the funds raised were used to treat alcoholics (November 1989). Religious artifacts were rediscovered and available for public viewing (November 1988). While under Brezhnev, charity would have been deemed unnecessary, under Gorbachev, the press increasingly featured those who were helping others. Irina, Sister of Charity, noted that the nuns all pray for perestroika, "because it has brought changes in our lives especially since the meeting of Pimen, Patriarch of all–Russia, with President Gorbachev" (January 1990:23). Idealistic culture, adopted from the West, included a shift from the group to the individual as the unit of analysis and as the measure of abstract ideals. For example, President Gorbachev argued in his report to the nineteenth party conference that the new socialism was "a system of true and tangible humanism in which the individual is really the measure of all things" (September 1988:4). Note that Gorbachev was referred to as president rather than General Secretary in the press after he gained that position along with that of general secretary. In a commentary on human rights, Oleg Shibko stated that:

> Whereas in the previous decades the main accent in the civil and political spheres was on citizen's duties to the state, now the emphasis is on duties of the state to ensure the rights of the individual. We have realized that the central aspect of the individual's relationship with society is personal sovereignty. (July 1989:3)

The Soviet press adopted many Western characteristics. Editor Robert Tsfasman, responding to a letter from an American suggesting that *Soviet Life* should not adopt Western styles, said he did not think the staff should try to make *Soviet Life* like other magazines. He noted that they were using reprints extensively because "our press and periodicals abound in frank and interesting articles." He added that "naturally, they are all written 'in the

Russian style'" (November 1988:1). Nevertheless, *Soviet Life* changed its format to resemble Western magazines. Western viewpoints were increasingly featured in Soviet publications, and Western publications became the model for many Soviet editors (January 1989). The public opinion poll emerged as a device for gauging the public's views and for reporting them in the press.

A new business culture used the vocabulary of capitalism. *Soviet Life* abounded with references to "cost–accounting," "self–financing," "efficiency," and "profit." *Soviet Life* espoused the ideals of individualism and hard work, offering adulation for the self–made man or woman (more often man), who was his or her own master. One article that reported the results of joint ventures noted that the American business community was ready to invest in the U.S.S.R., but that the Soviets had to put away their old methods. The author was happy that the Harvard Business School had offered to collaborate with Soviet research institutes "to work out the basics of management techniques for joint ventures" (January 1989:23).

Advertising was adopted as well; *Soviet Life* primarily featured ads for Intourist, Zig Zag, or other travel agencies. Business reforms were reported in the banking industry; Estonia was reported to have its own commercial bank—the first of its kind in the nation. This development was reported as being in line with Gorbachev's policy of decentralizing finances and promoting more creative banking (November 1989).

The March 1989 magazine cover featured a representative of the new Soviet culture, Yekaterina Chilichkina, the new Miss Europe. Soviet beauty contests had been initiated only recently. This Soviet beauty queen, when asked how she felt about being judged by her beauty, asked "What is wrong with a woman being recognized for her beauty?" (March 1989:31).

SUMMARY

The analysis of the Gorbachev era content of *Soviet Life* shows that media content and framing changed dramatically along with Gorbachev's reforms. Soviet society was more realistically presented, no longer as a model society, but as one fraught with social, economic, and political problems. The United States no longer represented the evil capitalistic society. The policies of perestroika, democratizatsiya, and glasnost promoted radical changes in Soviet society: the content of *Soviet Life* showed those changes emerging from previously suppressed cultural forms in the U.S.S.R. as well as from new, Western forms of culture.

Several themes were played out repeatedly in the magazine. Gorbachev's policies were presented as consistent with Leninist doctrine and as a return to the ideals of the October Revolution. *Soviet Life* purposively displayed the fruits of Gorbachev's policies. Perestroika, glasnost, and democratization were shown as being implemented and as working where they were allowed to flourish. At no time was any real challenge to Gorbachev's policies presented in *Soviet Life*; thus the magazine did not represent the full range of Soviet opinion.

While the other major Novosti publication, *Moscow News*, was controlled by the same agency, the newspaper's role was different. The newspaper was distributed abroad in English, but it served primarily as a tourist newspaper for visitors to the U.S.S.R. In the next chapter I will analyze the content of *Moscow News* under Brezhnev, in order to demonstrate the conservative role the paper played at that time. In chapter 6 I will compare this role under Brezhnev to that under Gorbachev, and demonstrate that *Moscow News* in contrast played a pivotal role in social change under Gorbachev.

6

News as Polemic: *Moscow News* under Brezhnev

As a magazine, *Soviet Life* was filled with colorful pictures and materials on the U.S.S.R. *Moscow News*, on the other hand was meant to be "news"— given the newspaper's role as an international newspaper and yet a promoter of Russia, what would the newspaper's contents be? How would the format reflect these purposes?

FORMAT AND STYLE OF *MOSCOW NEWS*

Words and sentences remained complex in *Moscow News* by American news standards. As was the case in *Soviet Life*, words were often more than two syllables in length and sentences very lengthy, perhaps due to the direct translation of the Russian language. The use of political labels was extensive: words such as fascists, imperialists, Zionists, and socialist internationalists were common.

SOURCES AND REPRINTS

A section of *Moscow News* was devoted to printing excerpts from other media sources, including those that were formally official, such as *Pravda*. This again highlights the relationship among Novosti Press Agency; the official press; the Communist Party; and the Soviet government. Rather than the newspaper competing with other Soviet newspapers, *Moscow News* used those papers as sources, reprinting their articles and utilizing their journalists. The newspaper's style would thus be like that of other Soviet newspapers: dour and bureaucratic. Who would read it?

MOSCOW NEWS' AUDIENCE

Moscow News differed from *Soviet Life* since it served as both a domestic and foreign publication. Therefore, the audience was more diverse, and the newspaper was geared toward reaching those within the Soviet Union, those in the United States, as well as those in other Western and non–Western countries. The paper's content under Brezhnev reflected this difference in audience, since the material was more polemical, brash, and overtly political. The newspaper was aimed toward readers who might be swayed toward the Soviet position on various policy issues, as well as toward the political leaders who were "conversed with" within the news columns.

ADVERTISING

Advertisements appeared intermittently in *Moscow News* during the 1972 to 1974 period; many ads featured technical services rather than products. Products that were advertised included camera lenses (December 2–9, 1972), shipping equipment (March 3–10, 1973), transistor radios (May 26–June 2, 1973), Russian vodka (May 26–June 2, 1973), and television sets (December 8–15, 1973). Export services appeared regularly in *Moscow News*, such as "Tsvestmetprom–export," which provided assistance in the constructing mineral processing facilities (June 24–July 1, 1972), and "Novoexport," which developed horticultural strategies and exported materials. A typical ad, such as the one for "Selkhoz Promexport" read:

> Renders technical assistance to foreign clients in the organization of timber–felling work, aforestation and the construction of enterprises for the woodworking industry. The machinery and equipment supplied are distinguished for their high quality of manufacture, and have an excellent record of operation under various climatic conditions. (February 3–10, 1973:15)

THE COVERAGE

Throughout this period, Y.A. Lomko served as editor in chief of *Moscow News;* but the Editor was never represented in the newspaper as a writer. Letters to the editor were printed without response. Several journalists reappeared, including the future, influential representative of the U.S.A./Canada Institute in Moscow under Gorbachev, Georgi Arbatov. Arbatov was featured as a commentator on U.S.–Soviet relations. Other regulars included Vasily Andrianov, Lev Volodin, Anatoly Belobrov, Vasily Kharkov, Dmitry Lobanov, and Albert Grogoryants, who appeared as political commentators for the paper.

A column by Natasha Zemlina called "The Way Natasha Sees It" interlaced the personal and the political much the same way Darya Nikolayeva's articles did in *Soviet Life*. Zemlina's column, entitled "Flowers of Life," discussed the daycare center where she took her son. She concluded that "A simple calculation shows that thanks to the care of the state a great many young Muscovites grow up in excellent conditions, and become hardened, strong, and healthy" (February 5–12, 1972:15).

THE CAST

The two most newsworthy figures during these years were Vladimir I. Lenin and Leonid I. Brezhnev. Government officials, such as then president of the Supreme Soviet Nikolai Podgorny, Foreign Minister Andrei Gromyko, and Alexei Kosygin, chairman of the U.S.S.R. Council of Ministers, were also featured prominently in *Moscow News* through their speeches and declarations as well as reports of their activities.

The characters and institutions reported on in *Moscow News* were presented as either allies of the Soviet state on policy issues or as people who were chastised and rhetorically challenged in defense of some allegation or another.

Individual American Allies

Those Americans who were represented as supporting Soviet policy positions included U.S. peace movement participants and labor union members. At the International Consultative Meeting for the World Congress of Peace Forces in Moscow, a representative from the U.S. People's Coalition for Peace and Justice claimed that the Vietnam War was far from over and resented that the U.S. peace movement was being belittled and blamed for the war (March 31–April 7, 1973).

The American vice president of the meat cutters and butchers union argued that the peace movement must do something about the number of hot spots around the world by bringing together people of different ideologies. U.S. labor union representatives also claimed that tremendous progress had been made in the Soviet Union where labor conditions were excellent. Delegates from the U.S. United Electrical Radio and Machine Workers said they would return to the United States and report on the Soviet Union's impressive labor policies to dispel the many misconceptions that existed (December 2–9, 1972).

Angela Davis, an American member of the Communist Party, was covered extensively for her mistreatment in the United States and her much hailed visit to the Soviet Union. An article called "Good–bye Angela" reported on Davis's visit to the U.S.S.R.:

> Everything we have seen here has exceeded our expectations ... It is difficult to express the depth and scope of the impressions which we picked up during the trip round the U.S.S.R. ... We were welcomed everywhere with love and friendly feelings ... Everything we saw inspired us, strengthened our loyalty to the causes of communism, and we are going back to our country full of impressions which will remain in our hearts forever. (September 23–20, 1972:8)

Moscow News announced that Soviet filmmakers were even producing a film about Davis.

Georgi Arbatov masterfully cited a number of Americans, including political leaders, successful business people, academicians, and military specialists, in an article on Soviet–American relations. In this piece Henry Kissinger was represented as supporting a policy of peaceful coexistence and quoted as stating that "power no longer translates automatically into influence" (April 28–May 5, 1973: Supp.). Kissinger was said to favor a transition to a new system of international relations that precluded the use of force; a position promoted by the U.S.S.R. (October 13–20, 1973).

Arbatov also cited L. B. Lundborg, former board chair of the Bank of America, as favoring a reduction of military spending and a pursuit of financial competition following the West German and Japanese models. Arbatov also referred to Richard Barnet, a social scientist, who stated that "since the mid–1960s, the cost of maintaining the imperial system began to outweigh the benefits," and that "corporate leaders, proceeding exclusively from economic criteria, were now concluding that promoting national interests using the armed forces posed a threat to their property and profits" (October 13–20, 1972:7)

General J. Gavin, a military specialist, was quoted as saying: "What is the basis of power in this kind of world? Can it be reckoned in terms of weapons? Number of divisions? Aircraft–carrier task forces? Or is it based on economic well being?" Each of these men was cited in support of Soviet policies and agendas.

Businessmen Cyrus Eaton, Dana McBarron, and Armand Hammer were also portrayed as friendly supporters eager to establish and broaden business relations with the U.S.S.R. Eaton was awarded the Lenin Prize for promoting international peace and for advocating open trade as a vehicle for better relations between the United States and the Soviet Union. Nelson Rockefeller was also quoted as arguing that trade should not be used as a weapon (October 13–20, 1973). Finally, a historical reference quoted Benjamin Franklin from the journal *Annual Studies of America;* it reprinted part of a letter he wrote to a Russian scientist showing his esteem for the work of Russian scientists (April 1–8, 1972).

Individual Allies Outside the United States

Those depicted as non–Western supporters of Soviet domestic and foreign policies included members of all Warsaw Pact countries, who were shown in complete agreement. Socialist countries were portrayed as allied on various issues (except China, which was accused of having perverted Marxism). Eric Honecker, First Secretary of the German Democratic Republic Central Committee, was bestowed with the Order of Lenin for his "great contribution to strengthening peace and socialism" (May 26–June 2, 1973:4). Other East bloc leaders recognized in *Moscow News* included Nikolae Ceausescu of Romania, Josip Broz Tito of Yugoslavia, L. Svoboda of Czechoslovakia, and the Bulgarian ambassador to the U.S.S.R. Dimitr Zhulev.

Particular leaders, such as President Ton Duc Thang of the Democratic Republic of Vietnam, Cuba's President O. Doricos, and President Saddam Hussein of Iraq, were shown as allied with the Soviet Union and as grateful beneficiaries of Soviet assistance in their struggles for justice. Support for Salvador Allende was evidenced in denouncements of "right–wing" attempts to overthrow the Chilean leader. *Moscow News* went so far as to declare that miners in Leningrad, aircraft workers in Kiev, electrical engineers in Riga, textile workers in Kirov were all meeting to condemn the junta's actions against Allende and to protest the arrest in Chile of Luis Corvalan, the general secretary of that nation's Communist Party (October 13–20, 1973).

Additional support for Soviet policies came in the "Letters to the Editor," all of which contained salutary greetings and positive commentary about the Soviet system. For example, a letter from Mohammad Terhouchi from Morocco states: "Your Soviet society is one of peace, democracy and equality. I am grateful to the Soviet Union for its tremendous efforts in support of the just struggle of the fighting peoples" (November 10–17, 1973:2).

Individual American Adversaries

Several figures in the United States were covered extensively in *Moscow News* as the deluded and corrupt nemeses of the Soviet Union.

According to the paper, these people opposed Soviet policies and misinformed the American public about the motives of the Soviet state and Communist Party. These leaders were shown to be interfering with the moral struggles being waged by Soviet client states against oppression.

The paper argued that U.N. Ambassador George Bush interfered with the right of African peoples to their sovereignty. According to *Moscow News:*

> Imperialists are making new steps toward a compromise with the white racists in the south of Africa. This precisely was the real aim of the recent tour of seven African countries made by Mr. Bush, the U.S. permanent representative to the United Nations Organization. Wherever he went, he sought to prove the impossibility of resolving the problems of racism and imperialism in Africa. (March 4–11, 1972:7)

Bush was also accused of obstructing Arab peoples' rights to their territories, since he opposed Iraqi President Saddam Hussein's demands for the United States to discontinue aid to Israel (March 4–11, 1972:7).

United States Senator Henry Jackson was depicted as being viciously anti–Soviet, discouraging Congress from pursuing arms control and trade agreements with the U.S.S.R. Jackson was described as an obstacle to free trade and to restructuring American foreign policy (October 13–20, 1973:6). The American who was attacked most severely, however, was Zbigniew Brzezinski for his criticism of Soviet society. In an article entitled "Sovietologist by Trade and Conjurer by Vocation" the paper claimed that:

> Zbigniew Brzezinski is an odious person. He stands alone, for his pathological hate of everything Soviet even among his other "Kremlinologists." This hate is obviously blinding for it prevents him to see the facts, so when Brzezinski starts to interpret the facts to suit his own ideology, he is forced sometimes to make capers worthy of a circus clown. Let's take, for example, one of his most recent columns published in the December 13, 1971, issue of *Newsweek* magazine, entitled "Trade and Ideology." Citing several utterly groundless figures on the "real" (sic!) Soviet defense spending (fantastically blown up in fact) and making a mysterious mention of nameless ringleaders of the Soviet "military–industrial complex" (sic!), he then proceeds to produce, like a conjurer pulling things out of a hat, his main egg—all shiny on the surface, but rotten inside—and

benignly allows Uncle Sam to trade with the U.S.S.R. But in so doing he condescendingly remarks that it would be of little advantage to the Americans, but the Russian would be in for trouble, because trade would be a sort of an "ideological yoke" around their necks (February 5–12, 1972:5).

The article then refutes the allegations made by Brzezinski in *Newsweek*.

Individual Adversaries Outside the United States

The character of the attacks made by *Moscow News* on adversaries was very defensive, as though the newspaper were actually responding to allegations posed by individuals. For example, Soviet dissident Andrei Sakharov received tremendous attention following his negative statements about the Soviet Union. An entire page of *Moscow News* was devoted to denouncing Sakharov and refuting his statements to the Western press. In a letter from members of the Soviet Academy of Sciences signed by 40 scientists, Sakharov's credibility as a scientist was questioned, along with his political motives:

A. D. Sakharov tries to justify these statements which are profoundly alien to the interests of all progressive people, by gross distortion of Soviet reality and false reproaches in relation to the socialist system. In his renouncements he, in fact, identifies himself with the most reactionary imperialist quarters which strongly oppose the line of peaceful coexistence of states with different social systems and are against our Party's and state's policy for the promotion of scientific and cultural cooperation and for stronger peace among nations.

Thereby A. D. Sakharov has actually become an instrument of hostile propaganda against the Soviet Union and other socialist countries. The activities of A. D. Sakharov are basically alien to Soviet scientists. They look particularly unseemly at a time when the efforts of all our people are concentrated on solving the grand tasks of the economic and cultural development of the U.S.S.R., on strengthening peace and improving the international situation.

We express our indignation at the statement by Academician A. D. Sakharov and strongly denounce his activity defaming the honour and dignity of a Soviet

scientist. We hope that Academician Sakharov will consider
his actions. (September 15–22, 1973:4)

Moscow News claimed that the Soviet public was outraged at Sakharov for
opposing détente in light of dangerous U.S.–Soviet tensions.

Institutional Allies: The U.N. and Foreign Press Organizations

Moscow News repeatedly called for compliance with United Nations
resolutions, particularly with regard to the Vietnam War and the Israeli–
Arab conflict. The paper claimed that the United States and Israel were
violating U.N. resolutions. In contrast, the Soviet Union was shown as the
initiator of many positive developments on the U.N. Security Council,
including a cease–fire agreement between Israel and the Arab nations
(November 10–17, 1973:6).

A letter to the editor from an American reader was said to represent
the reaction of *Moscow News* readers to the stand taken by the People's
Republic of China in the United Nations:

> At long last the People's Republic of China has been seated
> both in the United Nations and the U.N. Security Council
> for which the Soviet government and the Soviet U.N.
> delegation fought for many years. The question that now
> arises is: do the government of China and China's
> delegation to the U.N. understand the purport and the aims
> of the U.N. and its charters? Maybe they don't want to
> understand like the U.S. and British delegations? When the
> United Nations assembled for the regular autumn session
> and the Chinese delegation was seated the Soviet delegation
> put forward a proposal in favour of universal disarmament
> as it had done many times before. And what happened: The
> Chinese delegation, coming from a so–called socialist
> country, opposed the proposal and voted against it. What a
> shock. The Chinese leadership is going hand in glove with
> the imperialists who also oppose disarmament.
> —Karl G. Koch, U.S.A. (February 5–12, 1972:2)

In this manner, the U.S.S.R. was depicted as the nation truly allied with the
United Nations, while the "imperialists" corrupted the U.N.'s purpose.

The "imperialist powers, colonialists, and racists" were portrayed as
undermining the U.N.'s special investigation of problems in Africa as well.
Entitled "Operation Anti–U.N.," one *Moscow News* article described how the
Soviets applauded the activity of the "decolonization committee," whose

efforts regretfully were being undermined, "wrecking ... the U.N. decisions aimed at protecting African peoples' interests" (April 29–May 6, 1972:4).

While the *The Washington Post* was sometimes attacked for its material, it was also cited as supporting one Soviet position: its questioning of Israel's "right to continually occupy alien territories, provoke the vengeance of the Arabs and a dragged–out local conflict, and maintain the constant threat of third world war" (November 10–17, 1973:5).

The Christian Science Monitor was also cited about the United States' surprise at the time and place of an offensive launched by the People's Armed Forces of Liberation of South Vietnam (April 29–May 6, 1972). *The New York Times* was said to recognize that "Washington's promise to completely withdraw U.S. troops proved to be a mirage" (August 26–September 2, 1972:7). American journalist Eugene W. Moore wrote a piece for *Moscow News* about how poor the information was in the United States on the Soviet Union, and about how much he enjoyed his travels in Moscow (August 26–September 2, 1972).

Institutional Adversaries: Western Propaganda

Articles in *Moscow News* also attacked the press in other countries for printing articles that criticized the Soviet Union. For example, the French journal *Le Neaveau* was accused of printing misinformation about the Soviet policy of peaceful coexistence. *Le Neaveau* claimed that the policy was just a front for an aggressive Soviet foreign policy. *Moscow News* claimed this was all nonsense caused by those in the West who wanted to undermine Soviet–French détente. *The British Press* was attacked for portraying Soviet peace proposals as hidden and sinister, and The *London Daily Telegraph* was called an "Engineer of Provocation." According to *Moscow News*, the *Daily Telegraph*, closely allied with the Tory government:

> seems to be anxious to establish a new yellow press red–herring record. Of late it has been giving its pages frequently to colourful descriptions of 'a growing Soviet armed threat' to China ... Why should the life–wise British experts in ideological sabotage stoop so low? Things must be really bad with them. (February 5–12, 1972:2)

Both *The Washington Post* and the French newspaper *Le Figaro* were accused of undermining the Soviet–initiated Helsinki meetings on European security and of linking the conference with issues that should have been kept separate. *Newsweek* printed the article written by Brzezinski, reportedly "scaring" his readers with "fables about Soviet 'militarism'" (February 5–12, 1972:6).

The Voice of America, Radio Liberty, and Radio–Free Europe were described as propaganda centers in the West that engage "precisely in diverse ideological subversion against the countries of socialism while, according to the pronouncements of their bosses, their business is to facilitate a free exchange of information among nations'" (September 15–22, 1973:7). These organizations, which were labeled as Cold War instruments, were attacked repeatedly in *Moscow News* for creating problems between the Soviet Union and West Germany and China.

MEDIA FRAMES: DOMESTIC ISSUES

Moscow News presented highly polemical political material interspersed with articles similar to those in *Soviet Life* during this period. The newspaper presented the Soviet Union as remarkably democratic and attractive, particularly compared to the United States. As in *Soviet Life*, *Moscow News* described the U.S.S.R. as free of problems, including ethnic conflict, crime, unemployment, drugs, homelessness, and general social injustice. In other words, the domestic media frames described in *Soviet Life* operated in *Moscow News* but were not emphasized as much. This material read like a travel brochure, which one expects simply to sell the location in question. The emphasis on Brezhnev and Lenin found in *Soviet Life* during this period was also evident in *Moscow News* (see Figure 3).

Figure 3: References to General Secretaries, CPSU, *Moscow News*, 1972 and 1973

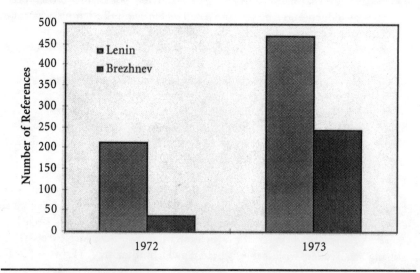

The Framing of International Relations

The focus of *Moscow News* was more overtly political than that of *Soviet Life* and in particular addressed problems of international relations. This material was organized around the following frames: 1. peace lovers and evil empires; 2. the less developed countries; and 3. the emerging world system of socialism frame.

Peace Lovers and Evil Empires

Soviet foreign policy, as presented in *Moscow News*, was directed at several key issues. Each foreign policy position was framed in terms of the Soviet Union's support for justice, peace, and freedom as compared to the United States and other oppressors. For example, Supreme Soviet Presidium President Nikolai Podgorny stated that:

> We have done and are continuing to do all we can to eliminate the dangerous hotbeds of imperialist aggression in Indochina and the Middle East, conditions for a stable peace on the Indian subcontinent have been created. The Soviet Union is resolutely opposed to the imperialist policy of wars and oppression, and advocated the final liquidation of colonialism and racism, the just settlement of international conflicts in the interests of the peoples, the ensuring of security in Europe and other regions, and the strengthening of peace on our planet. Our country's Leninist foreign policy is yielding undoubted positive results. (January 8–15, 1972:7)

This comparison often took the form of contrasting the NATO countries with the Warsaw Pact.

NATO, the Cold War, and European Security

Soviet foreign policy was said to be consistent with Lenin's policy of peaceful coexistence. The "Soviet peace offensive," however, was portrayed as difficult to pursue given the situation in Europe and around the globe. According to *Moscow News*, Europe—where two world wars were started—"remains a continent of great concentration of armed forces: those of the aggressive NATO bloc, on the one hand, and of the defensive Warsaw Treaty, on the other" (January 8–15, 1972:7).

Moscow News presented a consistent Soviet priority of developing some collective security arrangement in Europe, but argued that NATO opposed it. The Soviet Committee for European Security Deputy Chairman Nikolai Polyanov claimed that the "Atlantists" were supporters of the "small Europe of the six and of the nine" (December 2–9, 1972:5). NATO leaders were accused of pursuing a strategy not of European cooperation, but of enhancing NATO's power through military alliances and nuclear proliferation in Europe.

NATO leaders were shown to be undermining the Helsinki meetings by attempting to link European security issues with other matters. The "Atlantic" leaders were also accused of imparting a purely military character to the European conference, insisting that agreements on reducing armed forces and armaments be made as a precondition to the conference (December 30–January 6, 1973). In the final analysis, *Moscow News* argued, NATO leaders did not want peace to be ensured in Europe. International commentator Anatoly Belobrov argued that:

> The NATO strategists find it ever harder to come out openly against the steps motivated by the interests of peace and security in Europe. They have to resort to devious ways to blackmail and ideological sabotage in an attempt to impress upon the nations the need to build up the military potential of the North Atlantic bloc ... Every objectively thinking political leader in the West realizes the sheer absurdity of the plans and calculations, which are dictated by anything but genuine concern for European peace and security. (March 31–April 7, 1973:8)

Criticisms of the West were sometimes couched in more ambiguous terms, without referring to NATO or the United States. One article noted that the "enemies of the Soviet people" were distributing false information to try to sway public opinion in their favor. The "enemies" were said to fear the positive developments in Europe, as "the enemies of peace and progress always rear their heads when changes that favour cooperation and the security of nations begin to show" (December 30, 1972–January 6, 1973:5). After the first Conference on European Security and Cooperation had taken place in Helsinki, *Moscow News* supported a move to the second stage of the Helsinki meetings (December 8–15, 1973:7).

NATO countries were accused of maintaining the nuclear arms race despite Soviet efforts to end the Cold War. The contradiction between the changing situation in Europe and the positions of NATO leaders "who are openly pining for the times of the Cold War" was called the "NATO merry-go–round" (June 23–30, 1973:7). The heads of the U.S. military industrial complex were presented as unwilling to relinquish the Cold War framework, and "echoes for their calls for stepping up the arms race can be heard during Congress discussions of the Moscow strategic arms limitation agreements" (August 26–September 3, 1972:5). Georgi Arbatov claimed that, where nuclear weapons were concerned, "today perhaps only madmen in the United States can hope to unleash such a war and not to perish in it" (April 28–May 5, 1973: Supp.). Anuar Alimzhanov argued that the destruction from such a war would be horrible, given that Hiroshima and Nagasaki had served as "a rehearsal" (March 4–11, 1972:12).

Indochina

The war in Indochina was the international issue receiving the most attention. The president of the Democratic Republic of Vietnam, Ton Duc Thang, was interviewed in *Moscow News* in an article called "The People of Vietnam Will Win" (January 7–14, 1972:2). According to this article, the American imperialists were on the verge of defeat in Vietnam, but still refused to give up the fight. A cartoon in the March 4–11, 1972 issue showed an American plane with an eagle's head holding a bundle containing a missile in its beak. The bundle was inscribed with "new peace terms for Indochina."

A statement printed in *Moscow News* representing members of Soviet trade unions condemned U.S. aggression in Vietnam, Laos, and Cambodia. A Soviet "Week of Solidarity with the Struggle of the People of Vietnam Against U.S. Aggression" was declared (April 1–8, 1972:5). The newspaper described protests from all over the country in response to the mass bombing of the Democratic Republic of Vietnam and to the air raids on Hanoi and Haiphong. Soviet women were said to be particularly outraged (April 29–May 6, 1972). A reprinted TASS statement declared:

> Washington's decision to suspend the Paris talks for an indefinite time—all this is in irreconcilable contradiction to the official U.S. statements of a desire to achieve a peaceful settlement in this area. No false protests can conceal the fact that this is in fact a continuation and extension of the crimes of the U.S. military against the peoples of Indochina … It is absolutely clear that neither the military pressure, being carried out in the framework of the notorious policy of "Vietnamization" of the war, nor the new threats and provocations can break the will of the courageous Vietnamese people, the patriots of Laos and Cambodia who are waging a just struggle for their national rights, freedom, and independence. (April 29–May 6, 1972:4).

The TASS statement described the Soviet Union as invariably on the side of "heroic Vietnam" and demanded an end to U.S. bombings. With each escalation of the war, *Moscow News* printed a government statement calling for an end to the violence and declaring its continued support of the Vietnamese in accordance with the Soviet principle of socialist internationalism. Often these declarations were pronounced jointly with other countries, such as the Soviet–Yugoslav communiqué printed in a supplement to the June 24–July 1, 1972 issue.

The Vietnam issue was tied to a general notion that the United States was an evil aggressor. For example, one article featured the headline: "May the Tragedy of Khatyn Lodice, Oradour, Hiroshima and Son My Never Happen Again!" (July 29–August 5:11). The article indicted the United States for its imperialist, warlike behavior, and said the U.S. would have to admit that military means could not resolve the region's problems. A letter to the editor from a reader in India claimed that the whole world was watching the United States commit genocide in Vietnam (December 2–9, 1972).

The signing of the Paris Agreement to end the Vietnam War on January 27, 1973, was welcomed in *Moscow News*, and was followed by calls to strictly observe the agreement. The newspaper later claimed that the Saigon administration was violating the treaty and that no real cease–fire was occurring (April 28–May 5, 1973). Dangerous developments were reported such as the invasion of Cambodia by Saigon troops, backed by the United States. Satisfaction about the end of the Vietnam War was conveyed in the supplement to the December 8–15, 1973 issue of *Moscow News*.

The Middle East

The Middle East was described as the next major incendiary spot in the world at this time, again due to the irresponsible actions of the imperialists. The enemy in this foreign policy arena was Israel, which was backed by the United States. *Moscow News* regularly printed vitriolic assaults on "Zionism." A typical passage follows, in an article reprinted from *Izvestia* entitled "Zionism Is the Enemy of Freedom–Loving People:"

> Zionism is one of the forms of fascism. First of all, because such is its nature, such is the ideology and policy of the big Jewish bourgeoisie, which has established in Israel an open terrorist dictatorship for the most reactionary, most chauvinistic and most imperialistic elements of finance capital. Like all other extremist varieties of bourgeois nationalism, the Zionists allege that the nation is the supreme and extrahistorical form of social unity, binding

with blood kinship all the social strata imbued with a
harmonious community of interests ... Characteristically
enough, American Zionist gangs maintain the closest
relations with the ultra–right and openly fascist
organizations in that country. No wonder that those who
acted in complicity with the nazis are now ready to take
part in any crimes of American imperialism. (February 5–
12, 1972:5)

The initiation of an American military base in Greece provoked
further outrage since this was interpreted as a link in "Washington's overall
aggressive strategy" of suppressing the liberation struggles of the Arab
nations (March 4–11, 1972:5). *Moscow News* reported a session of the
General National Congress of the Arab Socialist Union in Cairo at which
Iraq's Saddam Hussein reaffirmed the "just stand of the Soviet Union on the
Middle East" (March 4–11, 1972:7). Israel and the United States were
denounced, and the unification of Arab states was proposed.

A Soviet–Iraq treaty was ratified, which expressed the friendly and
cooperative relationship between the states. The Soviet people were said to be
engaged in a powerful campaign of solidarity with the Arab peoples "in their
just anti–imperialist struggle against Israeli aggression and for freedom,
independence, peace and social progress" (June 24–July 1, 1972:3). According
to *Moscow News*, the task of setting up conditions that favored a peaceful
resolution of the Middle East conflict justified the supplying of weapons and
military training to Arab regimes. *Moscow News* stated:

We were of the opinion and still think that the struggle for a
political settlement is inseparable from the active trend
towards strengthening the combat ability of the Arab
countries. We are firmly convinced that the greater their
combat power, the nearer the political solution of the
Middle East problem. (June 24–July 1, 1972:3)

Moscow News expressed support for the decision of Iraq and Syria to
nationalize the Iraq Petroleum Company, even though this infuriated a
number of Western elites who had been profiting from the venture. The
Soviets claimed to support the right of the Iraqi people to the natural
resources of their land, through which they could improve their standard of
living (June 24–July 1, 1972). Letters to the editor from readers in Arab
countries regularly expressed thanks for the support of the Soviet state.

Following the Olympic games in Munich, *Moscow News* reported
that Israel had launched barbaric attacks against "neighboring countries"
that were reprisals for the killing of Israelis at the Munich games. The

newspaper claimed these incidents were not linked or justifiable: "The connection of hostilities launched against neighboring countries with an act of terrorism committed in Munich is a gross violation of international law" (September 23–30, 1972:7).

Israel, in its expansionist quest, was said to ignore both world opinion and U.N. demands to end the conflict (December 2–9, 1972; June 23–30, 1973; November 10–17, 1973; December 8–15, 1973). Eventually, a call to obey U.N. Resolution 242 was printed, urging Israel to cease occupying Arab lands (December 8–15, 1973). At times Israel was described as being backed by the United States, and at other times it was described as a tool of the United States. A declaration from the World Peace Council session condemned U.S. policy in the Middle East and argued that

> Israel receives the strongest backing of the U.S. Administration which is rendering her increasing political, economic and military support, turning Israel into an arsenal serving imperialist aims of supremacy in that part of the world, rich in power potential and of great strategic importance. The policy of backing Israel pursued with U.S. support, is aimed at suppressing the liberation movement of Arab peoples who are fighting for national independence and progress. (March 31–April 7, 1973:8)

A visit to the United States by Israeli Prime Minister Golda Meir, which produced more money and armaments to Israel, fueled Soviet outrage over the situation. *Moscow News* argued that U.S. policy in the Middle East was simply geared toward protecting U.S. interests (March 31–April 7, 1973). The oil crisis in the West was described as a tool the Arab nations could use to pressure the United States to stop supporting Israel's aggressive policy in the Middle East so that a peaceful settlement could be reached (December 8–15, 1973).

China

The People's Republic of China received enormous coverage in *Moscow News* as the nation that perverted Marxism–Leninism and "sold out" to the fascist/capitalist/imperialists. The Chinese leaders' actions were said to serve the interests of the "enemies of the peoples of the world" (February 5–12, 1972:2) and to be increasingly allied with "the opponents of détente." According to *Moscow News*, the Chinese obstructed the positive measures that were being considered by the United Nations General Assembly (October 21–29, 1972).

The "Your Questions Answered" section of the newspaper addressed a question said to come from readers in Algeria and Bangladesh: "What is Maoism and why is it incompatible with Marxism–Leninism?" (March 3–10, 1973:2). *Moscow News* defined Maoism as:

> not an independent or original doctrine, it may be defined as an eclectic system of views which attempts to bring together the traditional canons of Confucius, petty bourgeois ideas, extremely nationalistic concepts, and some Marxist propositions. ... For all that the Chinese leaders have been trying, already for more than a decade, to impose Maoism upon the international Communist movement, presenting it as the "only Marxist revolutionary theory" of our time. Peking propaganda dresses Maoism up in quasi-scientific attire, and strives to affirm some of its "ideas" by distorted propositions from Marxist–Leninist theory. (March 3–10, 1973:2)

The Soviet obsession with the Chinese was increasingly played out in *Moscow News*. A supplement to the September 15–22, 1973 edition devoted a full six pages to China in which China was accused of trying to claim the developing countries and of arousing suspicion against the Soviet Union. The Chinese were accused of making contact with extreme right–wing factions in the Federal Republic of Germany and with the Voice of America and Radio Free Europe in order to discredit Soviet policies. *Moscow News* claimed that "In this subversive activity the Maoists collaborate with the emigrant scum dreaming about the restoration of capitalism" (September 15–22, 1973: Supp.).

The Less Developed Countries

Moscow News defined the Soviet role in the Third World as that of the gracious ally and assistant to the less developed countries in their struggle for autonomy, economic development, and social justice. The countries (or peoples within them) that *Moscow News* claimed the Soviet Union was helping included Vietnam, Cambodia, Laos, Bangladesh, Rhodesia, India, Iraq, Morocco, Ethiopia, Guinea, Mozambique, Namibia, Angola, Zimbabwe, South Africa, Korea, Chile, Columbia, Iran, Nepal, Yemen, and Mexico.

For example, this effort to assist the developing countries struggling under the yoke of the oppressors included Chile, which was undergoing a right–wing coup d'état. It also included Africa, which was being exploited by the Portuguese. In letters to the editor, readers from each of these nations expressed their profound gratitude to the Soviet state and people for their support.

While the Soviets granted consistent and principled support to developing countries, *Moscow News* claimed that:

> The imperialists have turned the developing countries into "Cold War" battlefields to facilitate the preservation of their privileges and camouflage their colonialist designs. It was precisely in that period that imperialism had on many occasions used the military club against the peoples who were fighting for liberation from colonial and semi–colonial dependence. It was precisely in the "Cold War" years that military blocs were established in the Third World zone, blocs which became imperialism's weapon in the struggle against the national–liberation movements in the corresponding regions. (September 15–22, 1973: Supp.)

The newspaper ·argued that Washington enforced a brutal policy of promoting multinational corporations in the Third World, threatening these countries loan suspensions and trade restrictions if they refused to allow U.S. monopolies to exploit their resources (February 5–12, 1972).

Elements of Cooperation: Peaceful Coexistence, Détente, and Trade

Despite the caustic assaults on the capitalist countries and China, *Moscow News* presented the Soviet Union as following a consistent policy of peaceful coexistence, in line with Lenin's thinking. One of the startling features of *Moscow News* during this time was the juxtaposition of hostile material about "enemies" with material suggesting the prospects for increased trade and détente. This often took the form of a "buffer page" devoted to issues of cooperation between nations preceded and followed by incredibly contentious material on the United States or other enemy nations.

Grounded in Leninist thought, the Soviet Union's foreign policy was described as follows:

> beginning with the autumn day in 1917, when the people, led by the workers, captured power in Russia, has always been a policy of peace and international friendship, for freedom and independence, a policy of effective cooperation with all countries. Even in the opening days of the Soviet state, Lenin said " ... it is our duty to do everything that our diplomacy can do to relay the moment of war ... we

promise the workers and peasants to do all we can for peace." (January 8–15, 1972:7)

The only war the Soviet Union had entered since the Bolshevik Revolution that was mentioned in *Moscow News* was the Great Patriotic War, World War II, which was forced upon them in self–defense against the Nazis. This war was glorified repeatedly with reviews of the Battle of Stalingrad where the Nazis were defeated.

The policy of peaceful coexistence, which this coverage implied, was repeated throughout this time period, and *Moscow News* argued that the Soviet Union was living proof that Lenin's policy worked. *Moscow News* regularly printed articles calling on other nations to renounce the use of force, especially in Europe. This peace loving policy was said to be supported by worldwide public opinion. The Soviet Peace Committee, and the peace fund that subsidized it, was described as "a mass–scale, voluntary, public organization which could only be called an organization of the entire people" (December 2–9, 1972:6).

The newspaper claimed that trade was an effective means of achieving peace between states of different social systems. Via a statement by the Ministry of Foreign Trade (reprinted from *Trud)*, the newspaper expressed satisfaction that the United States and other NATO countries were removing trade barriers with the U.S.S.R. (March 4–11, 1972). United States President Richard Nixon was reported to be considering most–favored–nation trade status for the U.S.S.R. (April 28–May 5, 1973). A later issue of *Moscow News* promoted the development of long–term trade agreements between the superpowers. Academician Ivan Ivanov said that "we welcome the U.S.A. as a trading partner" (December 8–15, 1973:6).

Other material stressing cooperation between the United States and U.S.S.R. included articles on the successful conclusion of the Apollo 17 space mission, a joint flight that was represented as a milestone of Soviet–U.S. space cooperation.

According to Georgi Arbatov, however, the credit for improved relations between the United States and the U.S.S.R. rested squarely with the Soviet Communist Party and the increasing influence of socialism around the world, which had decreased tensions and violence globally (December 8–15, 1973: Supp.). The Soviets had broken through the Cold War, according to *Moscow News*, by initiating the policy of détente. With the change in the correlation of world forces, Arbatov claimed that the United States now realized that imperialism does not work.

The Emerging World System of Socialism

According to *Moscow News*, the global ascendancy of socialism was increasing dramatically, accompanied by a decline in influence of capitalism. Marxism, according to the director of Warsaw University's Institute of Philosophy, was the system best equipped for solving problems in the modern world (May 27–June 3, 1972). Letters to the editor argued that "the scales are tipping in favour of socialism" (June 24–July 1, 1972:2), and progress was assessed in all the socialist countries in their technological, economic, and social development. Reports from the Soviet Republics noted the dramatic advancements there since acquiring Republic status. In the words of one Georgian writer: "Lenin's words came true" (July 29–August 5, 1972:15). The Soviets had resolved the "nationalities question," according to *Moscow News*, unlike the United States, in which the melting pot theory had proven to be false.

Capitalism, with its reliance on exploitation and oppression, was described as declining. Several reports on the declining value of the U.S. dollar appeared in *Moscow News*. One article called the dollar a "chronic patient" and claimed that the imperialist policies pursued by the United States, the main "citadel of capitalism," caused the devaluation (May 27–June 3, 1972:7). The ruble, in contrast, was described as stable since "No inflationary trends exist in the Soviet Union. ... The fact that there is no deficit in the budget of the Soviet state is also a token of the stability of the Soviet ruble" (April 28–May 5, 1973:5).

The arms race was described as creating a deficit in the U.S. budget, accompanied by rising living costs, unemployment, and social inequality, thus aggravating conflict in the society. Lev Volodin claimed that the U.S. system "required a complete overhaul" (March 3–10, 1973:7). In sum, socialism was shown to be emerging as a world system with tremendous advantages over capitalism in providing for people's needs and in easing international tensions.

SUMMARY

During the Brezhnev years, *Moscow News* promoted the Soviet Union as an advanced, democratic nation in which Lenin's dream of socialism proved to be the correct path to follow. More important, *Moscow News* served as a forum for expressing Soviet positions on world affairs; this material remained central to the newspaper's content. *Moscow News* showed the Soviet Union pursuing the cause of justice and the liberation of oppressed peoples worldwide, whereas the United States and its allies were following the opposite course, especially in Vietnam and the Middle East. Because *Moscow*

News was produced for several publics, it was much more blatant and directly critical of the West than the more formal and diplomatic publication *Soviet Life*.

The newspaper attempted to serve as a forum for a "global conversation" by printing materials directed at policy makers and others, and thus influencing public opinion around world events. In the next chapter we will examine *Moscow News* under Gorbachev. As a venue for political communication, how would the paper serve Gorbachev? Would news continue as polemic regarding the East–West conflict?

7

Media Glasnost: *Moscow News* under Gorbachev

Under Gorbachev, bold political changes were introduced including a radical redirection of the media's role, as discussed in Chapters 1 and 2. *Moscow News* took on the special role as Gorbachev's advocate and was referred to by the Russians as "Gorbachev's newspaper." In this chapter we will examine the new *Moscow News*, to determine the efficacy of Gorbachev's policies of glasnost, perestroika, and democratizatsiya. How would the new policies be reflected and constructed through the newspaper?

A NEW VERBAL STYLE

Moscow News shed much of the terse language that characterized the paper during earlier years, although it did assume that readers had sufficient knowledge of the political and economic problems facing the country to understand specialized articles by academicians.

New words were popularized, including the language of the market—"cost accounting," "self–financing," even the words "profit" and "competition" were introduced. The term "charity" was used as well, even though it had in the past been declared as an unnecessary bourgeois tool to pacify the working class in capitalist countries. Another important term introduced in the press under Gorbachev was "public opinion."

Words that declined in usage include acceleration (since the economy was not improving); political labels also diminished, with almost no references to Zionists, imperialists, fascists, socialist internationalism, socialist humanism, socialist realism, and the bourgeoisie.

CHANGING NEWS TOOLS

Public opinion was recognized as a powerful force for creating social change. This led to the use of opinion polls conducted by *Moscow News'* own sociological service, the Academy of Sciences, and even those done by the international Gallup organization.

Moscow News features acquired the quality of investigative reporting in which journalists showed their commitment to getting at the "truth" and uncovering instances of injustice that should be rectified. These stories are described in the section on human rights. Glasnost allowed the emergence of political satire in Soviet publications. Leonid Treyer wrote regularly for *Moscow News* under the column "Topical Satire." Wit and somberness characterized Treyer's satire; his articles poked fun at Russian "national character" and simultaneously humiliated those individuals who opposed reform, albeit by indifference rather than active opposition. For example, on the psychological difficulties citizens felt with the removal of wage leveling and socialist distribution, Treyer mocked "I'd rather suck my thumb from hunger than die of envy for my neighbor" (May 21–28, 1989:10).

While Soviet news did not develop the sensationalism of U.S. news, several stories resembled the kinds of events that make news in the United States. For example, it was reported that a woman set herself on fire in front of the Kremlin and died (June 19–26, 1988), and that a plane hijacking had ended in bloodshed (March 27–April 3, 1988). These kinds of stories would not have been included in the news under Brezhnev. The hijacking story received complete and prompt coverage in *Izvestia* and *Pravda* as well, marking a first for the Soviet official press.

THE PRESS' ROLE

Both Novosti Press Agency and *Moscow News* were involved in activities that departed from journalism. Novosti actually organized workshops where democratic principles were taught: A game was invented called "District Election Meeting" in which mock elections were held, and players tried to implement democratic practices while legal experts coached them on how they should act under the law (January 8–15, 1989). Novosti also organized roundtable discussions on issues of concern; this was a part of its revised 1986 charter.

Moscow News advertised a "hot line" for readers to report any information about organized crime, a "cancer" that it claimed could only be cured by joint efforts. The newspaper staff promised to investigate the crimes and "publish the facts" (September 10–17, 1989:15). While this could be classified as investigative reporting, it overlaps with the stated goal of punishing criminal activities.

SOURCES AND REPRINTS

Moscow News continued printing some pieces from *Izvestia, Pravda,* and other publications, but generally only as small excerpts followed by a response to the article. The "interchange" with other publications now took the form of an extended conversation in print rather than simply reprinted material. For example, an article written for *Izvestia* might be critiqued in an opinion piece in *Ogonyok,* followed by a *Moscow News* article containing a rebuttal from the person who originally wrote for *Izvestia.* The "global conversation" thus developed within the U.S.S.R. as well with dialogue taking place through various domestic papers.

THE AUDIENCE

Under Gorbachev *Moscow News* oriented toward the domestic customer. While the audience still included an international readership, the newspaper's content addressed domestic problems and their prospective solutions. Letters to the editor came primarily from domestic readers and addressed domestic issues. Intellectuals were the newspaper's primary contributors and also seemed to be the most important consumers, since intellectuals, the government, and party leadership conversed and debated through the press. Its advertising made it clear, however, that the newspaper still addressed the peoples in the West, especially business and government figures.

Advertisements became a regular feature of *Moscow News* during this period. These ads, geared toward the Western consumer, most commonly featured industrial services and products. *Moscow News* intermittently carried a "Special Supplement for Businessmen," which featured ten or eleven pages of advertisements and services that promoted joint ventures. One of the more innovative advertisements featured a large photograph of Ronald Reagan and Mikhail Gorbachev signing the INF (Intermediate Range Nuclear Forces) treaty with the large headline "The Pen Is Mightier than the Sword." Below the photo the virtues of Parker pens were espoused. *Moscow News* noted that two million people in the U.S.S.R. and one and a half billion people abroad read the ad.

An interesting addition to the newspaper was an ad for the Poisk (Search) cooperative, which appealed to the consumer who had not yet "found [your] family happiness" (April 23–30, 1989:4). For $50, one could state his or her romantic desires for a lifelong mate in a column called "Let's

Get to Know Each Other." While an ad from a Swedish male followed the initial advertisement for the service, no further ads appeared in subsequent issues indicating the service's lack of popularity or perhaps an editorial change.

THE CAST:
THE GOOD, THE BAD, AND THE REHABILITATED

The people covered in *Moscow News* represented various groups including: 1. progressives, hallmarked by Lenin and Gorbachev; 2. conservatives (including Stalin, Brezhnev, and their remnants), the "old thinkers," and the conservatives in the West; and 3. those individuals who were recently rehabilitated or who deserved recognition.

The Good: Progressives

Progressives wrote most of the material for *Moscow News*. They advocated a return to Lenin's true policies, which Gorbachev was trying to reinstate. As in prior publications, Lenin received enormous attention and was referenced more than Gorbachev (see Figure 4). Lenin and Gorbachev were the most important figures but the members of the radical wing of the Congress of People's Deputies, called "The Interregional Group," were also heralded as forward–thinkers who could resurrect the Soviet economy. Workers involved in cooperative enterprises represented the antithesis of Brezhnevism, since they had somehow retained their entrepreneurial sense and ability to think independently. Perestroika would be built by such individuals, according to *Moscow News*.

Figure 4: References to General Secretaries, CPSU, *Moscow News*, 1988 and 1989

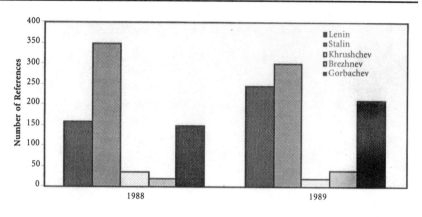

The Bad: Conservatives

The mascots of Soviet conservatism included Stalin and Brezhnev, whose policies had so deeply perverted Soviet society that citizens had become lazy and irresponsible, and bureaucrats had gained control of every aspect of life. *Moscow News* addressed some who still defended Stalinism, including the "ideal type" neoStalinist, Nina Andreyeva. Andreyeva wrote a defense of Stalin for *Sovietskaya Rossiya,* which then became a topic of discussion in many Soviet periodicals, including *Moscow News* (January 8–15, 1989). Progressives referred to Andreyeva's work as an "antiperestroika manifesto," which represented the threat of a return to authoritarianism (January 8–15, 1989). Editorial comments in *Moscow News* indicated that her position was an unpopular, minority position with which *"MN* disagrees" (October 9–16, 1988:2).

Moscow News indicted not only Soviet conservatives, but conservatives worldwide—one writer jokingly commented "conservatives of the world, unite!" (January 8–15, 1989:7). The ultra–right in the United States and the Soviet conservatives were depicted as dependent on each other for survival and thus unwilling to let go of the "enemy images" of the respective rival superpower. The conservative wing of the American press was referred to as "Stone–Age gospel;" conservative writers such as Pat Buchanan, William Safire, and James Kilpatrick were its "prophets" (September 11–18, 1988:1).

The Rehabilitated

Most figures reinstated to Soviet history, since they had been banned from the historical record under Stalin or Brezhnev, were now revered martyrs. Andrei Sakharov received accolades in the press, and a *Moscow News* opinion poll indicated that the citizenry held him in high regard, as did members of the Academy of Sciences and Congress of People's Deputies (November 6–13, 1988). Sakharov did have enemies among conservatives, evidenced by the fact that someone switched off the microphone seven times at the Congress of People's Deputies while Gorbachev was in the process of relinquishing it to Sakharov (July 16–23, 1989).

Nevertheless, *Moscow News* called for some caution and objectivity about the reexamination of historical figures and presented Trotsky, Bukharin, and even Trotsky's assassin, Ramon Mercader, as complicated individuals with good and bad traits.

The Coverage

During this time, Yegor Yakovlev served as editor in chief. He also wrote regularly for *Moscow News* and inserted editorial comments following various articles as well as a featured column called "Talking it Over With the Editor in Chief" in which he interviewed people and discussed various issues. Yakovlev's presence was strongly felt.

The *Moscow News* staff was presented as a united front on issues of social relevance. The newspaper regularly featured comments stating *"MN's"* position on an issue, giving the paper a lifelike quality, as though it could think and take a stand. Articles for *Moscow News* were written by many different people, mostly academicians and members of the Congress of Peoples' Deputies, the popularly elected representatives, many of whom were fervent advocates of Gorbachev's programs. There were journalists whose writing reappeared including Yakovlev and the two chairmen of the Novosti board, Valentin Falin and Albert Vlasov.

Women were very rarely featured writers in *Moscow News*, except for one–third of the "three authors" columns, called "My View." This is significant because women very rarely wrote commentary on international affairs or even domestic politics; rather, they generally wrote literary criticism or social commentary.

Spartak Beglov, the Novosti journalist who criticized the United States during the Brezhnev era, retained that role in the Gorbachev years and wrote almost all the critical articles on the United States, with particular attention to military policy.

Several foreign journalists and scholars contributed to the *Moscow News* during this period. Professor Marshal Goldman of Wellesley College and the Harvard Russian Research Center wrote a piece on how to salvage the Soviet economy, as did Stephen Handelman of *The Toronto Star*. The executive editor of *The New York Times,* A. M. Rosenthal, wrote a piece condemning Soviet officials for mistreating political prisoners. Robert Scheer of *The Los Angeles Times* contributed an article on the decline of American conservatism (particularly anti–Sovietism); Sovietologist Stephen Cohen wrote on the rehabilitation of Bukharin; John Keegan, *The London Daily Telegraph* defense correspondent, wrote on Soviet military forces in Europe; and Hedrick Smith, journalist and author of *The Russians* and *The New Russians*, declared his support for perestroika.

Robert Manoff, from the New York–based Center for War, Peace, and the News Media, was interviewed about "enemy images," and Richard Carlson, director of the Voice of America, was interviewed by Vladimir Pozner about freedom of information. Ronald Reagan wrote a piece saying goodbye and thanking the Soviets for their hospitality during his and Nancy Reagan's visit. George Bush contributed his condolences for the Armenian earthquake and claimed his son would visit Armenia at Christmas time to offer support.

MEDIA FRAMES

The material in *Moscow News* criticized social conditions and promoted Gorbachev's programs, particularly the one that had made the least headway thus far—perestroika. Significant attention was devoted to filling in "blank spots" in history and debating Stalin's role in Soviet history.

The following media frames emerged during this period: 1. social samo–kritika; 2. Gorbachev's promoter; 3. remnants of the East–West conflict; and 4. elements of discontent.

Moscow News as Social Samo–Kritika

One *Moscow News* reporter interviewed a cab driver about his thoughts concerning the fact that so much anti–Soviet material appeared in the press today. When the reporter asked what he meant by the term anti–Soviet, the cab driver replied, "well, the plain truth of course" (March 27–April 3, 1988:9). By filling in the "blank spots" in history, delineating various Soviet social problems, recording roundtable discussions, and printing editorials and political satire, the *Moscow News* editors devoted most of the newspaper's content to samo–kritika, or self criticism. Most of the analysis focused on domestic issues, since foreign policy remained a sensitive area still subject to censorship. The *MN* staff also stressed the urgency of resolving economic problems, without which the reform process might end and even reverse.

Domestic Criticism: Bureaucrats

Most of the domestic policy criticism was levied at problems resulting from the Stalin and Brezhnev eras. During the years of centralized management, bureaucratic inefficiency seemed to have penetrated every aspect of Soviet life, having attained an inertia that was almost impossible to overturn. *Moscow News* regularly featured articles calling for the removal of bureaucrats from the economy and administration. Bureaucrats were indicted in various articles for their unrealistic state orders of car batteries from factories (March 1–7, 1988), for failing to serve the people (July 17–24, 1988), for maintaining cultural mediocrity (September 10–17, 1989), for causing the recent physical tragedies in the Soviet Union (with which perhaps "the Almighty" was punishing the negligent) (June 18–25, 1989), for covering up the effects of the Chernobyl disaster (February 26–March 5, 1989), for undermining democratic electoral processes (March 26–April 2, 1989), and for subverting perestroika, glasnost, and democratizatsiya on the whole (January 8–15, 1989; January 22, 1989).

Compounding the problem, according to Alexander Trepelev, who wrote a piece called "Allow Me Not to Let You" (January 31–February 7, 1988), was the fact that bureaucrats were in charge of teaching democracy to the rest of society. Georgi Matyuknin agreed with Trepelev, and noted that the figures for the administrative cuts required by perestroika were set by bureaucrats themselves, who should be replaced with non–bureaucrats (March 1–7, 1988).

Reconstructing History

Columns called "Glimpses of the Past" and "Learning from History" were filled with debates over Stalin's emergence as Soviet leader. The fundamental question was whether Stalin was an evil man who cunningly gained control of the Communist Party as Lenin lay on his death bed, or whether he was an inevitable product of the Soviet social system. L. Lopatnikov wrote that any weak social system may opt for dictatorship, and "there's no use trying to sell the idea that dictatorship is 'inevitable under communism'" (July 17–24, 1988:2).

Len Karpinsky responded to an article by Alexander Tsipko in *Nauka I Zhizn* (Science and Life) that argued that theoretical connections exist between Marxism and Stalinism; Tsipko compared the phenomenon to a malignant tumor. Karpinsky insisted that Stalinism did not stem from Marxism, but did note that "new theoretical approaches" had come under consideration (April 23–30, 1989:9). This article implied that Marxism–Leninism was subject to criticism.

The Economy

The Soviet economy was a shambles, and *Moscow News* thoroughly described the complexity of the problem. The economic disaster involved Communist Party bureaucrats, excessive ministerial control, workers who had no incentives, shoddy materials and consumer goods, noncompetitive markets, an inconvertible ruble, and a social ethic that resisted the stratification that might result from the development of entrepreneurs. *Moscow News'* writers claimed that bureaucrats and "old thinkers" hindered economic recovery by undermining the cooperative movement and by resisting the market system (September 11–18, 1988; May 21–28, 1989; November 5–12, 1989).

The Environment

Moscow News argued that the inept management of the economy had led to the destruction of environmental resources, including the Aral Sea. Nuclear power was attacked as an energy source, given the atrocity of the Chernobyl disaster that was further exposed in the newspaper. Vladimir Kolinko wrote that the radiation levels in the Chernobyl area were still high, yet people were drinking milk and eating produce from the area. Although freak pigs and calves were being born, people were still not being given complete information or compensation for the damage done (February 26–March 5, 1989). In a later article, three scientists criticized the *Moscow News* report as sensational, but the editorial comments which followed explained that the public was not convinced by these "expert opinions" (June 18–25, 1989).

Crime, Discrimination, Unemployment

Many social problems previously assumed not to exist were covered, including an escalating violent crime rate and juvenile delinquency (June 18–25, 1989), the anti–Semitism of the Pamyat (Memory) Society (August 14–21, 1988), unemployment (September 10–17, 1989), and discrimination against women. *Moscow News* regularly featured a column called "She and We," which addressed problems of women in Soviet society, including data on abortions (January 22, 1989), poor medical care for pregnant women (April 23–30, 1989), the "double duty" of Soviet women in the domestic and career sectors (November 6–13, 1988), the objectification of women (June 18–25, 1989), and women's lack of political representation (June 19–25,

1989). Inna Vasilkova argued that journalism "is missing out a lot by being almost completely a male domain" (November 6–13, 1988:12).

Human Rights

Moscow News criticized earlier notions of human rights in the Soviet Union and described violations of those rights. A. Ivanov wrote in a letter to the editor that the right to work really meant the obligation to work, "since its corollary, the right not to work, does not exist" (January 10–17, 1988:2). Ivanov called for the deletion of the article on parasitism from the Soviet criminal code. Journalists began acting as investigative reporters, delving into stories about groups and individuals who deserved justice. For example, *Moscow News* investigated a case about a clergy member who was taxed unfairly (March 27–April 3, 1988); a case of foreign students who had poor mail service, were not given keys to their rooms, and were barred from traveling abroad during vacations (March 27–April 3, 1988); a case of a man who was unjustly framed and expelled from the party (March 26–April 2, 1989); and a case of a poor, old, crippled man who was rendered homeless by the housing office (March 26-April 2, 1989).

One official's role in building a state farm near Chernobyl was investigated by *Moscow News*, but the newspaper had not gotten an interview with the man. Editor in chief Yegor Yakovlev noted that he wanted to interview G. Tarazevich, the president of the Presidium of the Belorussian Soviet Socialist Republic Supreme Soviet, and added "we hope that G. Tarazevich will not skirt these issues" (December 3–10, 1989:15).

At times an authoritative figure from outside the U.S.S.R. was utilized to express dismay at human rights violations. Great Britain's secretary of state for foreign and commonwealth affairs said, in an interview, that those who wished to emigrate from the Soviet Union should be allowed to leave (January 10–17, 1988). *Moscow News* included several writings on the right of individuals to criticize their society, particularly in the context of Gorbachev's "new thinking." In fact, Mikhail Gorbachev's closing speech at the nineteenth All–Union Party Conference was reprinted in *Moscow News*, calling for people to learn the habit of criticism, "the habit of comradely polemic" (July 17–24, 1988:Supp.).

Letters published in *The New York Times* were summarized and reprinted in *Moscow News* about the ill treatment of prisoners of conscience and calling for an end to the imprisoning of dissidents (June 19–26, 1988). Use of the Soviet militia against demonstrating crowds in Tbilisi was criticized in *Moscow News*, and Gorbachev was shown to have lost some credibility due to this action (December 3–10, 1989); but Defense Minister Yazov refuted the charges that the public was sprayed with poisonous gasses. *Moscow News* argued that samples of the gas indicated that chlorofoss, a chemical used to exterminate cockroaches, was included in the mixture (June 18–25, 1989).

The use of the militia to prevent a demonstration organized to commemorate the 1968 invasion of Czechoslovakia also received attention from *Moscow News*. After interviewing experts and participants, commentator Leonid Miloslavsky said that the law must be obeyed, but should not be interpreted in a one–sided manner allowing for undemocratic groups like the Pamyat (Memory) Society to meet, but banning a democratic demonstration (September 11–18, 1988).

Moscow News established a clear position on religious freedom. Several articles dealt with the Ukrainians' desire to reclaim churches that had been converted to Russian Orthodox churches. Alexander Mineyev argued that the Ukrainian Catholic Church should be legalized and "given an equal place with the other twenty–three religious confessions registered in the U.S.S.R. *MN* is for all people being able to decide for themselves how to worship God, so long as their methods don't threaten the peace of others" (December 3–10, 1989:13).

A new individual right explored in the press was one's right to "be rich." Ilya Vais reported that a family's home had been searched by authorities, who discovered that the family had more clothes in the closet than the average citizen. The man was accused of speculation and given a criminal trial, despite the lack of any evidence other than the family's possession of too many goods (January 10–17, 1988).

The K.G.B.

Even the K.G.B. was criticized by *Moscow News*. Mikhail Shevelev wrote an account of how the KGB harassed him after he refused to be recruited as an informer (January 7–14, 1990). *The London Times* correspondent Christopher Walker warned that the ratio of KGB operatives employed for every foreigner living in Moscow was 14 to 1. Walker said: "ask any of the Western ambassadors here, what they associate with Novosti, and to a man they will reply K.G.B." (October 9–16, 1988:5).

Moscow News sarcastically suggested that Walker bring in twenty million foreigners to outnumber the K.G.B., but another piece by Nikolai Smirnov gave some credence to Walker's article. Smirnov explained that Philip Taubman, head of the Moscow office of *The New York Times*, was harassed by the K.G.B. Smirnov noted that Taubman "was frightened by tan Zhiguli cars, men in black raincoats, and crackling noises in his receiver," and Smirnov expressed his sorrow that the community of Soviet journalists had "failed to protect Philip Taubman," since eventually Mrs. Taubman was accused of harboring contraband at airport customs (August 14–21, 1988:13).

Censorship

Finally, secrecy and censorship were attacked as remnants of old thinking that were being maintained by a persistent party bureaucracy, including many holdovers from the Brezhnev era. Even military secrecy drew criticism. In an opinion piece, Yevgeny Gontmakher asked why army information was kept secret from Soviet citizens. Gontmakher complained that one must rely on the U.S.–published *World Almanac* to discover that the U.S.S.R. has the biggest army in the world. Genrikh Borovik also wrote that better information was needed about the Soviet military. He bemoaned the fact that "statistics covering certain quantitative characteristics of Soviet armaments are quoted in Soviet newspapers with reference to Western sources," and that "Soviet people have for years known the Soviet RSD–10 missiles by the Western name, SS–20" (March 27–April 3, 1988:3).

Richard Carlson of the Voice of America claimed that Radio Moscow was still broadcasting preposterous stories, including one that accused the United States of creating the AIDS virus. Carlson did note that he was surprised by *Moscow News'* critical coverage (January 10–17, 1988). Alexei Izymov argued that glasnost had not come to fruition in the economic sphere either. Economic statistics, also suppressed and distorted since Stalin, were still censored (July 17–24, 1988). While television documentaries had been decreed free of censorship, Lydia Polskaya reported that films were still being "shelved." The newspaper reported that "telephone games" continued; in other words, party officials prevented certain films from being shown (July 17–24, 1988; January 22, 1989).

One item of good news included a report that reliable maps of Moscow were being sold in bookstores for the first time in a decade. According to *Moscow News*, "previous maps–diagrams were published with considerable distortions introduced deliberately for the sake of secrecy which had become senseless already long ago" (July 16–23, 1989:14).

Foreign Affairs

Criticism of foreign affairs initially took the form of historical scrutiny, which attacked Stalin's and Brezhnev's policies rather than current policies. For example, the Soviet invasions of Czechoslovakia, the Ukraine, and Afghanistan were criticized in early editions of the paper. Late in 1989 criticisms of foreign policy became more frequent and detailed. Criticism of foreign policies addressed the following areas: 1. foreign debt and the failure to trade on the global market; 2. the failure to condemn inhumane acts; and 3. militarism.

Foreign Debt and Trade

Economist Boris Fyodorov noted that in the past, the press "loved to discuss the U.S. foreign debt, Mexico's foreign debt, and the foreign debt of many other countries, but we never said anything about our own" (November 6–13, 1988:7). The implication, according to Fyodorov, was that the Soviet Union had no foreign debt, but the enormous military spending of the state had produced a massive Soviet foreign debt and budget deficit. Fyatoslava Fyodorov thought the Soviet Union should enter *The Guinness Book of World Records* for being the most massive country to abstain from foreign trade for sixty years. He noted that many years had passed since Lenin advised the Bolsheviks to learn how to trade, and that perhaps his wish could finally be fulfilled (December 3–10, 1989).

Official Silence

The most robust critique of foreign policy appeared in *Moscow News* in the August 13–20, 1989, issue. Alexei Izyumov and Andrei Kortunov refuted Soviet Foreign Minister Shevardnadze's statement that Soviet foreign policy was deeply moral. Instead, they claimed that officials proclaimed moral principles in foreign policy but did not always implement them. The authors argued that the Soviets failed to condemn the inhumane policies of foreign states, including Iran's death sentence on Salman Rushdie, Romania's cruel treatment of the Hungarian minority, Manuel Noriega's corruption in Panama, and the Chinese tragedy in Tiananmen Square.

Izvestia political analyst Alexander Bovin expressed shame that Moscow kept silent on the Rushdie affair in order to maintain diplomatic ties with Iran (March 26–April 2, 1989). "Moral control" had to be increased by a free and independent press, which Izyumov and Kortunov claimed still did not exist in the Soviet Union, particularly regarding the censorship of international journalism.

Militarism

Moscow News devoted significant attention to criticizing nuclear weapons policies of the past. Pyotr Gladkov wrote a severe critique of Soviet participation in the arms race:

> Let's see what we've achieved by arming to the teeth. Our friends and allies are economically poor states. The military support we give them costs us a pretty "kopek" which could very well be used for our own needs. ... Let's imagine for a moment that America decided to invade the U.S.S.R. What

would it get? A vast country in economic shambles, with a
flimsy and morally retrograde technical base and
contaminated environment, a population most of which
has unlearned how to work, and ethnic conflicts any one of
which could lead to civil war. (September 10–17, 1989:6)

Ales Adamovich declared, after the signing of the INF treaty, that
"everything that has been accumulated in the name of mutual annihilation"
was "the most senseless goal in history" (January 10–17, 1988:6). Alexei
Pankin and Major Mikhail Smagin criticized the viability of deterrence, "the
cornerstone of the nuclear world's somber edifice," as a security system, and
agreed that a nuclear free future is possible (May 22–29, 1988:7).

Printed debates and roundtable discussions served as a venue for
outlining issues of controversy in the press. British journalist John Keegan
and Soviet historian Lev Semenko debated the progress being made on the
demilitarization of Europe. Keegan argued that the Soviets must make
significant cuts in conventional forces, while Semenko argued that Soviet
tanks were obsolete anyway, and that NATO must discontinue the
modernization of nuclear weapons while calling for conventional cuts
(March 27–April 3, 1988).

Another debate between Josef Joffe, the chief of the international
news department at Germany's *Sud Deutche Zeitung,* and Soviet historian
Lev Semenko examined the concept of "reasonable sufficiency" in defense.
Joffe claimed the Soviets should reduce their conventional forces to parity
with NATO, and orient them defensively rather than offensively to gain the
trust of the West (January 8–15, 1989).

A series of articles raised the controversial proposition that the
U.S.S.R. should convert to a militia–only defense force. This notion was
introduced by a letter to the editor from Lieutenant Colonel Savinkin, and
further developed by philosopher and Lieutenant Colonel in the reserves Igor
Shatilo. Shatilo argued that this was in fact Lenin's idea, and he went on to
advocate demilitarization:

> Any massive development of the "man–killing" industry
> quickly brings civilization closer to military self–destruction
> or to economic depletion which can, even without a war,
> bleed our planet white. To prevent this impending disaster,
> it is necessary to start everywhere limiting and cutting
> permanent armies, replacing them with a militia defense
> system. (January 2, 1989:4)

The army was also criticized as undemocratic, and rife with "hazing" and "fagging" (April 23–30, 1989:12). Georgi Arbatov explained that "old thinking" had become the main threat to security (January 10–17, 1988:6).

Dr. Bernard Lown, co–president of International Physicians to Prevent Nuclear War, presented the case that military spending had resulted in a national debt and shameful social consequences in both the United States and the Soviet Union, while Germany and Japan had prospered in the absence of nuclear weapons spending. Lown called for reduced defense spending and the allocation of resources for treating the sick and hungry and for saving the environment (January 22, 1989).

After opening a branch in Leningrad, a Greenpeace representative interviewed for *Moscow News* declared the group's opposition to Soviet nuclear vessels in the Baltic Sea. But the Soviet branch leader of Greenpeace claimed to have learned this only the night before the press conference (August 13–20, 1989).

Yuli Krelin argued that militarism had not only affected the Soviet economy, environment, and social sphere but had permeated the national spirit as well. Krelin went so far as to condemn the shooting down of Korean Airline flight 007 as "the permanent preoccupation with competition in the military sphere ... made us swallow the doctrinaire explanation of the need to down a South Korean liner without so much as an apology for the unpremeditated murder of civilians" (July 16–23, 1989:3).

Moscow News as Gorbachev's Promoter

The promotion of Gorbachev's policies accompanied *Moscow News'* criticism of Soviet society, since his reforms were designed to reverse the decline of the economy and other social malaise. The newspaper thus played out its historical role of collective propagandist, but glasnost brought a new dimension to the news. In the past, this role meant noncriticism of the Soviet leadership and misinformation about the state of the economy, the society, and the happiness of Soviet citizens. Under Gorbachev, the mobilization of support for perestroika was consistent with a sober analysis of social conditions.

Perestroika

Central to promoting Gorbachev's reforms was the notion that Gorbachev had reinstated Lenin's directives about the revolution. In fact, perestroika, the revolution, and socialism became equivalent in the press. The objectives of perestroika, according to Alla Gracheva, had much in common with the revolutionary agenda: "to rebuild everything ... to renew everything so that the mendacious, dirty, dull and ugly life of ours becomes just, clean, joyful, and beautiful" (January 31–February 7, 1988:13).

Moscow News addressed the idea raised in a *Wall Street Journal* article that the Soviet Union had forsaken Marxism–Leninism. Perestroika was not to be mistaken for a turn away from socialism toward capitalism; rather:

> Perestroika deals with the historical destinies of socialism in its historical competition against capitalism, and in ... its advantages, its ability to secure a higher than under capitalism labour productivity, and a level of people's well–being that corresponds to it. To do that, socialism must acquire a new quality (January 10–17, 1988:3).

Yegor Yakovlev further noted that the mass movement for perestroika "is being likened more and more often to the legendary times of the October Revolution" (August 14–21, 1988:3).

Responding to an article by Sovietologist Marshall Goldman, who recommended several market–oriented measures to rescue the Soviet economy, professor Erik Pletnyov responded that "the aim is to restructure socialism, not restore capitalism." Pletnyov rejected not only the "ideological" nature of Goldman's argument, but also the idea that "there should be voluntary re–establishment of exploitation of hired labour by private capital" (April 24–May 1, 1986:6). Pletnyov claimed that Soviet citizens would never tolerate such a system and were determined to carry out perestroika, or restructuring of socialism.

Gavriil Popov (later mayor of Moscow) argued that in studying the Chinese experience, one must conclude that Marxist principles have to work in combination with the specific cultural characteristics of any society. This analysis stands in stark contrast to the denouncements of the Chinese perversion of socialism expressed during the Brezhnev era.

In fact, economic restructuring was already achieving some successes in the Soviet Union, according to *Moscow News*. The city of Togliatti, where Lada cars are produced, had switched to a cost accounting system. According to the paper, "the city is saying goodbye to wage–leveling because it wants to live better and have a higher standard of living" (January 31–February 7, 1988:8).

On the whole, *Moscow News* presented a realistic assessment of the state of the Soviet economy, but one article resembled the Brezhnev era declarations of economic prosperity. The piece addressed Gorbachev's visit to Uzbekistan where, according to Vladimir Simonov, "under the family contract system, seventy percent of the income earned by collective farmers goes into their own pockets" (April 24–May 1, 1988:4). The difference between this article and Brezhnev era pronouncements, of course, is the emphasis on individual attainment.

Moscow News held up the cooperative system as the model of economic recovery. It seemed that by establishing such enterprises, initiative and hard work could bring profit and a renewal of the economy without exploiting people. Without some incentive or investment in one's workplace or product, the Soviet Union would continue producing shoddy goods and poor services.

People were called upon to act on behalf of their country. Grigory Kanovich told readers not to wait for someone else to repair the country, saying that "A slave always waits. A free person acts, instead of standing on the shore" (April 24–May 1, 1988:4). Vitaly Tretyakov, in presenting a portrait of a "typical Soviet family," argued that "their future depends on how actively they promote democratization in society" (May 22–29, 1988:8). The most blatant manipulation of public opinion appeared in the February 26–March 5, 1989, issue, in which an opinion survey was printed, followed by *MN* political analyst Vitaly Tretyakov's statement that:

> In the editor's views, the election platform of our paper's readers, formulated on the basis of their replies to a questionnaire, testifies: *MN* readers are fully in favour of perestroika which should be carried out as fast as possible and be very radical, a perestroika carried out in a forthright and democratic way, in the interest of people, for the sake of building a democratic socialist society committed to the rule of law. (p. 9)

The survey included biased questions such as "What elements of the command–and–administer system still continue to exist?" and "What must be done without delay to eliminate these obstacles in the way of perestroika?" (February 26–March 5, 1989:9).

Democratization

Moscow News presented the Communist Party as an institution which needed fundamental reform; the success of perestroika relied on political reform. For example, the Ministry of Finance prevented cooperatives from surviving by levying huge taxes on them. Party members refused to adopt democratic procedures and practices because it would mean losing control and privileges.

Yegor Yakovlev explained that in Lenin's last "Letter to Congress," written on his death bed, he called for changes in party structure and democratization; Gorbachev was simply carrying out Lenin's wish (April 24–

May 1, 1988). Alexander Bovin argued that the democratization of the Party involved a "strict observance of Leninist principles and standards of party life;" eliminating the centralized methods of decisionmaking and issuing orders; increasing the "efficacy of Party propaganda;" enhancing the role of mass media in the processes of democratization and glasnost; and bringing institutions and leading personnel in line with the law (March 27–April 3, 1988:8).

Despite allegations that the party and government were undemocratic, *Moscow News* never argued for a multiparty system, suggesting a remaining "forbidden zone" of coverage. Yuri Burtin argued that because the Central Committee is not popularly elected, the body is not in line with democratization; but he claimed that the possibilities for democratization under a one party system had not yet been exhausted (May 22–29, 1988).

Expanding the Limits of Glasnost

A telephone survey of 400 Muscovites (by *MN's* sociological service) found that sixty–four percent of the respondents trusted the newspaper (May 22–29, 1988). Yegor Yakovlev, editor in chief of *Moscow News,* proudly stated that his job is glasnost, and that he endured criticism from the party for discussing sensitive matters in the paper (March 26–April 2, 1989). In addition to delving into previously "forbidden zones" of media coverage, the newspaper addressed the issue of glasnost regularly, and writers called for censorship to be completely eliminated.

Alexander Bovin wrote an article called "Let's Break the Ice on Foreign Policy," which suggested that perhaps journalists could criticize in that sphere as well (June 19–26, 1988). Two historians called for a law on freedom of information and said that the Soviets could learn from the U.S. experience (September 10–17, 1989). The boldest article addressing the problem of glasnost included a very detailed draft law that would abolish censorship. The article, entitled "Journalistic Fantasies," was simply signed "A Journalist" (October 8–15, 1989:10).

Remnants of East–West Conflict

Moscow News carried a great deal of critical material about the United States; it was geared toward promoting Gorbachev's policy of reversing the nuclear arms race and of pressuring the United States to cease its intervention in the Middle East and Latin America. It focused especially on the U.S. role in the nuclear arms race.

The Arms Race

Moscow News articles criticized conservatives in the United States for trying to block the INF treaty and for resurrecting the "evil empire" image of the Soviet Union. Oliver North and Dan Quayle were indicted for their cynical attacks on the Soviet Union and for North's use of patriotism to justify the Iran Contra scandal (February 26–March 5, 1989). Jack Kemp was chastised for accusing the U.S.S.R. of breaching the INF treaty and for forging photographs and statistics (January 31–February 7, 1988).

The newspaper printed regular INF updates that bemoaned the procrastination of the disarmament process. Spartak Beglov accused the NATO countries of paying "lip service" to the INF treaty; he complained that while Ronald Reagan voiced support for a nuclear free world, his closest ally, Margaret Thatcher, claimed that a nuclear–free world would be dangerous and impossible (March 1–8, 1988:3). The French government was also criticized for its enormous military spending simultaneous with opinion polls that indicated that French citizens increasingly believed the U.S.S.R. was devoted to peace (May 21–28, 1989:2).

Even after the ratification of the INF treaty, Valentin Falin, then Chair of the Novosti Press Agency board of directors, argued that the United States was stalling on an agreement for fifty percent reductions in nuclear weapons. "The stubborn aspiration to leave loopholes so that the arms race reduction and real disarmament in one field can be turned into the development of the arms race in other fields is a well–known confirmation of America's plans" (June 19–26, 1988:3).

The U.S. refusal to link arms reductions with the ABM (anti–ballistic missile) treaty and with a nuclear test ban attracted criticism from *Moscow News* writers. Vladimir Nazarenko accused the United States of stalling on an agreement and insisted that the Soviet side was "ready for the next round of talks" (July 17–24, 1988:5). Nazarenko appeared to have the authority to speak for the Soviet government. In that same issue, deputy minister of foreign affairs Vladimir Petrovsky outlined the "sticking points" for the United States on reaching a disarmament agreement at the U.N. General Assembly. Petrovsky indicated that all delegations agreed to the plan except the United States which, in placing its own interests above those of international disarmament, "did not behave as a participant in a democratic, civilized dialogue should" (July 17–24, 1988:6). When the United States still had not agreed to Soviet initiatives in August 1988, Spartak Beglov claimed that "as for disarmament, the NATO policy is lame on both feet" (August 14–21, 1988:5).

Gennadi Gerasimov denounced Henry Kissinger for his skepticism about Soviet proposals, even while Kissinger acknowledged that Gorbachev was serious and the West must formulate a response. Gerasimov again emphasized that the Soviet Union was waiting for the West to join the Soviet Union in the disarmament process (January 8–15, 1989). Spartak Beglov argued that the U.S. delay was due to the American vested interest in maintaining the Cold War framework, so that U.S. nuclear missiles could be placed in West Germany in the name of NATO unity (May 21–28, 1989). Beglov accused James Baker of concealing this U.S. vested interest by claiming there was no proof that Brezhnevism had been repudiated. This continual prompting of the United States was headlined with titles such as "Waiting for the West's Yes" and "Waiting for the Next Step ... This Time from NATO."

U.S. Interventionism

In a story in a *Moscow News* supplement about a meeting between Mikhail Gorbachev and Jordan's King Hussein, both leaders called for an international conference on the Middle East in which the PLO would participate. Gorbachev complained that "there are doubts as to whether those who speak for embargo the loudest and who, by the way, were caught at secretly supplying arms to Iran will be observing the embargo ... the Soviet Union does not supply arms to Iran" (January 10–17, 1988: Supp.).

The U.S. strategic alliance with Israel was also criticized as a militaristic policy that prevented a Middle East settlement (March 1–7, 1988). According to writer Karen Khachaturov, this policy had fueled the continuation of the Iran–Iraq war, and threatened the entire Persian Gulf region. The author argued that the Soviet settlement of the Afghanistan war could become a model for resolving the problems in the Middle East (April 24–May 1, 1988). Afghan army General Ziarmal, in an interview with *Moscow News*, claimed that the United States had broken its commitment to a political settlement in Afghanistan by supplying Pakistan's army with weapons after the Soviet withdrawal (October 9–16, 1988).

The U.S. exploitation of Latin America in general was criticized by journalist Vitaly Kobysh, who said that the Soviet Union should help those countries and expressed hope that the United States would not be threatened by such action (November 6–13, 1988). Spartak Beglov, in his column entitled "If One Is Not a Diplomat," attacked the U.S. intervention in Panama and criticized the discourse of U.S. policymakers that sought to disguise the reality of American intentions. Beglov cited terms and phrases such as "intervention," "to protect the lives and property of American citizens," and "requests from governments for help," as the inventions of a militaristic society. According to Beglov, "'regular exercises' is, perhaps, the most fortunate linguistic find yet" (April 24–May 1, 1988:5).

Elements of Discontent

Despite the overwhelming support for Gorbachev's policies expressed in *Moscow News* during this period, frictions began emerging between: 1. Novosti Press Agency officials and the *Moscow News* staff; and 2. the *Moscow News* cadre and Mikhail Gorbachev.

Novosti Press Agency and *Moscow News*

The difference in tone between articles written for *Moscow News* by the respective chairmen of the board of directors of APN, Valentin Falin and Albert Vlasov, and the rest of the *MN* staff showed that the chairmen followed the more conservative party line. For example, Vlasov wrote a piece on Tiananmen Square in which he claimed the United States had too hastily condemned the Chinese government (June 18–25, 1989), while *MN* journalists denounced the action in later articles.

A *Moscow News* article by Vyacheslav Dashichev, about Stalin's wicked intentions to capitalize on Nazism to inflame tensions in Europe so that communism would exert wider appeal, created a stir. Novosti Press Agency printed a statement in *Pravda* denouncing the article. It contended that:

> Novosti Press Agency cannot but express absolute disagreement with the *MN* publication. As Publishers of *Moscow News,* the Agency hereby express bewilderment over the fact that the editors had not bothered to study the matter deeply and consequently misled their readers, and showed lack of respect for historical facts (*Pravda,* August 26, 1989).

By printing this statement in *Pravda,* APN revealed its ties to Soviet officialdom, while the *Moscow News* staff further severed its historic links to the Party. *Moscow News* printed a response to the statement claiming that, while the article did represent an opinion, the article was historically grounded and the opinion was shared by many Western scholars, such as Robert Tucker (September 10–17, 1989).

Moscow News and Gorbachev

While the early coverage of Gorbachev extolled his virtues, the first mention of Boris Yeltsin in *Moscow News* came from Gorbachev's statement at the nineteenth Party Conference in which he denounced Yeltsin for resorting to command methods at the Moscow city committee. Gorbachev quoted from the transcript of an October 1987 Plenary Committee meeting where Yeltsin admitted his errors (July 17–24, 1988:Supp.).

In late March 1989, however, *Moscow News* printed a brief defense of Yeltsin, who was being harassed at District Party Committee meetings where someone passed out pamphlets defaming him. *Moscow News* journalist Vera Gornostayeva asked "Who's behind it?" (March 26–April 2, 1989:4). The first printing of Yeltsin's views on the Interregional Group of People's Deputies contained the following:

> The inter–regional group has brought together those deputies who are not content with *perestroika's* tempo, its half–hearted measures in politics, the economy, the nationalities issues and the social sphere—the measures that have brought our country to the verge of crisis. (August 13–20, 1989: 8)

A brief report in *Moscow News* noted that Yeltsin contributed his royalties from his U.S. tour to combat AIDS but was followed by a report that the Better World Society had given its annual award to Gorbachev (October 8–15, 1989). Commentary about Gorbachev became mixed with positive comments and criticism. An ambiguous article on perestroika by Otto Lacis noted that "A leader must also be competent. And not all of our leaders have as yet shown that they are" (October 8–15, 1989:9).

The final article on Gorbachev in this sample, by Vitaly Tretyakov, described him as an enigma. The photograph of Gorbachev showed him covering his face, while the bold headline read:

> Perestroika marches on, and the flow of critical arrows flying at Gorbachev keeps on mounting. The pricks are increasingly more painful—there is no hiding this. And judging by his psychological frame of mind, it seems that he is not particularly able to hide this. Yet he has continued marching. Whither? Why doesn't he turn? And someone would ask: Why is he zigzagging? (December 3–10, 1989:9–10)

The author ended the provocative article with the question: "Do we and Gorbachev understand each other?"

SUMMARY

Under Gorbachev, *Moscow News,* headed by radical liberal and Gorbachev ally, Yegor Yakovlev, developed into a venue for social criticism and for the promotion of Gorbachev's reform policies. By the end of 1989, however, some disillusionment with Gorbachev emerged among the progressives on the newspaper staff as well as a growing distance between the newspaper and its publisher, Novosti Press Agency. Despite this apparent friction, *Moscow News* retained its status as a radical, highly political publication that promoted the democratization of Soviet society, with or without Mikhail Gorbachev as its leader.

Glasnost progressed sufficiently that the press, while not free of censorship or party interference, had considerable autonomy and popular support both in the Soviet Union and abroad. *Moscow News'* status as a radical newspaper suggests that it had some measure of power, since the non–Soviet world (particularly "Kremlin–watchers") would label any decline in press freedom as a turnabout in Soviet politics and a reversal of the reform process. Such perceptions could have resulted in the withdrawal of much–needed international support for the Soviet Union's economic development and could have rekindled Cold War tensions.

In the next chapter we will discuss the implications of Novosti Press Agency's work and that of its two major publications for the dissolution of the Soviet Union. We will consider the ambiguities inherent in attempting to use the media to impose change from above.

8

Reinventing the Soviet Self

Q: What do you need glasnost for?
A: To know which things are wrong in the generally
      right course.
—A Soviet and American student, discussing the media vis–
à–vis the government. (*Moscow News*, May 22–29, 1988:11)

Impression management dominated the mass media agenda in the Soviet Union during both the Brezhnev and Gorbachev periods of analysis. Under Gorbachev, however, glasnost allowed the development of a radical intelligentsia committed to broad scale social change. The radicals helped the manufacturing of dissent that was integral to Gorbachev's early success; the "elective affinity" between Gorbachev's interests and liberal ideas provided his basis of support. While the press was successful in removing the obstacles in Gorbachev's way, the boundaries of dissent continually shifted until eventually Gorbachev himself became an object of criticism.

Despite the pressures imposed on the mass media to respect the journalistic boundaries imposed by party conservatives, the radical intelligentsia pressed forward and ultimately developed an independent press. Members of the liberal press assert their political perspectives and continue advocating reforms, including the development of a market economy, democratic legal practices, and the expansion of human freedom. The reform media, therefore, assumes a political position and publishes persuasive materials. The difference lies in the fact that those materials are not bounded by the political leadership; rather, they express the thinking of intellectuals who seek social change.

MANUFACTURING DISSENT

Dramatic changes occurred in the Soviet mass media system under Gorbachev. Under Brezhnev, in contrast, mass media organizations were kept busy convincing the domestic and international public that Soviet socialism worked—the economy flourished, social problems were nonexistent, and people were happy. While, according to the press, Soviet citizens enjoyed their harmonious society, they expressed unanimous outrage at the Western imperialists for intervening in the Third World. The profit motive in the United States was presented as the evil drive that promoted imperialism and mercilessly pushed the world toward nuclear annihilation.

While "public opinion" was said to emerge under Gorbachev, it was fabricated under Brezhnev to mobilize acquiescence to the actions of the Soviet state and hostility toward the West. Public opinion assumed a new face under Gorbachev and was recognized as a powerful force in world politics. It could now be measured and presented back to the public via the opinion poll adopted from the Western press. These new Novosti opinion polls manipulated public opinion to demonstrate dissent, defining public attitudes that opposed the doctrines of bureaucratic authoritarianism; in other words, dissent was manufactured.

The "new thinking" imposed new organizing frames: even manufactured dissent was bound to suit the purposes not only of party elites but also of reform–minded people who wanted to mobilize support for democratizing the society. The prevailing definition of the national situation portrayed a society in a state of complete renewal—filling in gaps in history, soberly examining the results of the Stalin and Brezhnev years, rediscovering Lenin's true theories, and implementing them. The Soviet media missions of kritika and samo–kritika were introduced for the first time since Khrushchev's brief and limited "thaw." Collective agitation and propaganda remained central to the mass media's purpose; only the policies they advocated had changed.

The press under Gorbachev criticized the state of the economy, crime, and other social malaise, but certain zones of political life were still immune from examination. Novosti journalists, particularly those at *Moscow News*, cautiously entered the zones of foreign policy, Gorbachev's performance, and finally, alternative leadership.

THE LENINIZATION OF LEADERSHIP

While the media performed its cathartic function and convinced the international public that a new Soviet Union was evolving, it reassured the domestic public that Vladimir Ilyich Lenin would not lose his place in their city squares. Both Brezhnev and Gorbachev grounded their thinking and policies in the writings of Lenin; however, those writings were used to justify radically different policies. The press under Gorbachev never addressed this contradiction; it assumed that Gorbachev was Lenin's actual heir apparent.

Both General Secretaries Brezhnev and Gorbachev embraced, in theory, Lenin's policy of peaceful coexistence, his nationalities policy, and his concept of the Communist Party as the political vanguard. Under Gorbachev, a return to Lenin's New Economic Policy rationalized Gorbachev's overtures to a market economy, and Lenin's last letter to the Party Congress validated Gorbachev's attempts to reform the party.

Journalists, academicians, and political figures also cited Lenin's works when making an argument for reform. The centrality of Lenin to Soviet political culture since the Bolshevik Revolution demanded a recognition by everyone in the political arena; Soviet society was built on Lenin's ideas. The implicit rejection of so many foundations of Soviet life under Gorbachev had already left the citizenry without a framework of meaning; the banishment of Lenin would result in a complete cultural and political breakdown.

A NEW FACE: MARKET–CULTURE MEDIA

To captivate foreign readers and show them that the Soviet Union was truly changing, the media required a new face. The new image was developed not simply through strategic impression management; but rather, by adopting Western styles of media presentation, Novosti signaled its entry into the sphere of competitive journalism. *Soviet Life* changed in size; it included fantastic photographs and snappier headlines. *Moscow News* adopted color print and borders, controversial stories, and its journalists plunged headlong into the role of investigative reporting.

These strategies worked. The "toilet paper" *Moscow News* of the 1970s became Moscow's most demanded newspaper, so much so that the paper acquired black market status, leasing for exorbitant prices. People would actually lease the paper and return it for another reader to lease. The paper was reportedly selling out within ten minutes at local Soviet kiosks. Internationally, *Moscow News* developed its radical reputation so completely that it became one of the most reputable sources of information.

Soviet Life, as a diplomatic publication, maintained a less controversial presence, remaining outside the discouraged arenas of coverage. According to *Soviet Life's* subscription department, the magazine's popularity grew in the United States, particularly among individual subscribers and secondary schools, as a source of information and pictures of the Soviet regions.

Advertising proliferated in *Moscow News* so dramatically so that a supplement to the paper featured advertisements only. These supplements were often sold separately in the Soviet Union; one report indicated that eighty percent of domestic customers bought the supplement to read the business ads (*Moscow News*, March 1–8, 1988). Advertisements served two key functions for the newspaper; they promoted joint–ventures and foreign investment in Soviet enterprises necessary for developing a market economy, and generated funds that were needed, in particular, when *Moscow News* became an independent newspaper. This independence gave the newspaper staff a direct stake in increasing their circulation for the first time (*Moscow News*, September 23–30, 1990).

THE SOVIET COLLAPSE

Developments toward the end of Gorbachev's leadership demonstrated a split between Novosti Press Agency (it ceased to be called Novosti News Agency) and its publication, *Moscow News*, as well as continuing friction between Mikhail Gorbachev and his progressive "team." Tensions escalated between Communist Party conservatives and the reform–minded journalists, academicians, and politicians who supported a market economy, democratization, and press freedom.

THE *MOSCOW NEWS* AND NOVOSTI SPLIT

Near the end of 1990, Novosti Press Agency announced that it would no longer provide printing facilities or other support for *Moscow News*. According to editor in chief Yegor Yakovlev, Central Committee conservatives exerted their influence to deprive the newspaper of resources (*Moscow News*, August 16–23, 1990). In the Soviet Union, paper and printing facilities are scarce commodities for publishers; generally the state determines the allotment for a given periodical. Yegor Yakovlev appealed to readers, paper suppliers, and printers for support, and the paper was transferred to a joint stock ownership. The *Moscow News* building was then gutted by fire, and Yakovlev again appealed to readers for help and received many donations from inside and outside the Soviet Union. The newspaper printed notices of thanks to contributors.

The September 23–30, 1990 issue of *Moscow News* announced that it would begin its seventh decade fully independent of any state or party organs. Dmitry Mamleyev, first vice chairman of the state committee of the U.S.S.R. for the press, gave Yegor Yakovlev a new registration certificate for the paper indicating its independent status. According to the *Moscow News* report of this event: "From now on the only things higher than the convictions of *MN* journalists are the Law and the will of the founders—the representatives of the country's democratic public who have set up the '*MN*–People's Newspaper' Society" (*Moscow News*, September 13–20:2).

Moscow News joined with four other independent publications to form "The Forum Group." This group was devised to cover the activities of the Congress of People's Deputies Interregional Group's meetings of democratic parties and movements. Furthermore, it was designed to turn the independent democratic press into a "pressure group to urge the democratic parties and movements to come together on the basis of pluralism, and to seek consensus through compromise" (*Moscow News*, September 30–October 7, 1990:1). The forum included alternative newspapers in Kazan, Riga, Vilnius, Leningrad, and Moscow. Despite internal pressures, the independent press continued publishing radical material that criticized Gorbachev's conservative political shift.

Meanwhile, *Soviet Life*, which continued being published by Novosti and edited by Robert Tsfasman, remained true to the spirit of bounded glasnost. For example, the April 1991 issue contained frank and critical essays about the Soviet economy and violent crime and even discussed the West's growing suspicion of Gorbachev. But in the magazine's commentary section, centrist Igor Drobyshev argued that Gorbachev was not drifting toward the right and that he had exercised flexibility toward the Lithuanian independence movement. Drobyshev argued that "radicals have latched on to their hobbyhorse ... chanting that 'Democracy is in danger!' at meetings and in the 'radical press'" (*Soviet Life*, April 1991:2). He claimed that the left–wing democrats were actually responsible for discrediting democratic ideas. *Soviet Life* clung to its birthright, convincing the American readership that all was well in the U.S.S.R.

GORBACHEV AND THE RADICALS

While Mikhail Gorbachev confused the world with his shift back to the political "center," disillusioned reformists renounced their loyalty to the leader. Eduard Shevardnadze resigned as foreign minister, and Alexander Yakovlev, the powerful reform spokesman who many believe was the force behind democratization, resigned his post as chief of the CPSU Central Committee Propaganda Department.

At a gathering of Yegor Yakovlev (no relation to Alexander) and his compatriots to celebrate his sixtieth birthday, the mood was described by Yakovlev's son, Volodia:

> They just sat there, not talking, as if it were a wake ... They realized their dream was lost. They'd all quit Gorbachev and

the Party. They were in opposition to the man they had put all their hopes in. They were like believers who were suddenly made to realize that there is no God. (Remnick, 1991:1)

This group included reporter Alexander Bovin, sociologist Tatyana Zaslavskaya, historian Yuri Afanasyev, and other perestroishchiks who wrote for *Moscow News* as Gorbachev supporters but later wrote against him. Yegor Yakovlev claimed that "Gorbachev hates us now. ... When he says our name in public now, he uses the English—*Moscow News* instead of *Moskovskiye Novosti*—so that people will somehow brand us a paper of 'foreign ideas'" (Remnick, 1991:1). Once skeptical of Boris Yeltsin, these reformers turned to him in hope of greater flexibility and change.

ADMINISTERING GLASNOST OUT OF EXISTENCE

The passage of the law on the press in August 1990 was followed by a number of regulations that undermined it. The Council of Ministers restored the censorship of official media through "temporary" regulations. Regional and city newspapers were pressured to register their publications as party newspapers, thereby exposing them again to party censorship. Official newspapers were again subject to manipulation by the Communist Party leadership, which can call for the resignation of a troublesome editor in chief. Independent newspapers such as *Moscow News* were threatened with huge taxes and other economic sanctions, such as being charged outrageous prices for newsprint that is sold to the official papers for much less (*Moscow News*, February 10–17, 1991). Some printing shops refused to print unofficial newspapers; thus local officials could exert pressure to drive the publications out of business.

Other rules imposed on Soviet radio and television undermined the democratization process. A presidential decree narrowly defining democratization gave censors the right to obstruct the airing of unsavory content. Another regulation required television and radio stations to register with the State Committee for Television and Radio Broadcasting and with the Ministries of Justice and Communications. These organizations are known for adhering to old dogmas and practices.

THE FUTURE

Now that glasnost has evolved, can the proverbial genie be put back in the bottle? I have argued here that the mass media serve not simply to mirror reality but to actively construct reality, thereby shaping society and playing a role in defining the course of history. The question remains, how powerful a force are the media in influencing society's direction?

In the process of constructing new discourses, the old ones have been subverted. Can those old discourses be resurrected? Not completely. Glasnost is a frail creature as shown by the ease with which the Communist Party retracted the law on press freedom under Gorbachev. Conservatives in Russia may reinstate censorship and harass the independent press by denying them access to newsprint, but they cannot take back the contributions of the reformers. Not only did media frames and boundaries change, but new cultural norms, structures, and interrelationships emerged. Glasnost became sufficiently institutionalized and mature to remain a significant force, although not without challenges, in the former Soviet Union.

In the case of Soviet mass media, those who constructed the news were reflexive in their work; in attempting to manage impressions, they carefully manipulated the news to produce a certain desired outcome: the advancement of Marxism–Leninism and the pacification of the people. In participating in the construction of a certain definition of Soviet society, it appears that many of the manipulators actually came to believe that vision. The promoters began to accept that reality until Gorbachev began his "revolution from above."

Ironically, Lenin's concept of the press as "collective propagandist" may have been the very element that undermined its role in the Soviet Union. First, the direction of the news produced within this reflexive framework kept changing. Different leaders issued varying directives about what the press should accomplish. The shift from Stalin's "iron fist," to Khrushchev's somewhat increased openness, back to Brezhnev's conservative policies, and eventually to the radical policy turnabout under Gorbachev, produced unanticipated results. Suddenly, editors and journalists were told that their role was to criticize, to reveal the truth about conditions in Soviet society (within certain limits). The press, rather than serving the interests of the state and stability, actually sowed some of the seeds of discontent in the Soviet Union. As they moved toward investigative journalism, reporters exposed the reality that their own work had historically served the Communist Party.

Looking back at the party's role in manipulating public opinion, the contradictions inherent in presenting the news over time became apparent. The result was ambivalence and anger on the part of many, as reflected in letters to the editor over the media's exposure of the Soviet social malaise.

Recent changes in Soviet mass media, and in the former Soviet Union generally, reflect the impact of using dissent as a tool in managing impressions. While this strategy was very successful for Gorbachev in the early years of his leadership, eventually it turned against him. While dissent can be manufactured, and partly manipulated, the manufacturer only has limited control over dissent once it is unleashed. Gorbachev was "too successful" at manufacturing dissent; that dissent took on a life of its own, moving beyond the narrow purposes for which it was created.

MEDIA AND THE SOCIAL CONSTRUCTION OF REALITY

What then, can we conclude about the relationship between mass media and international relations? First, the fundamental sociological maxim, "Where you stand depends on where you sit" should be applied to institutions as well as individuals. This idea is not new, and is reflected in research on American mass media as well, even though the American and Soviet social systems are very different.

A sociological theory of mass media should include the following elements:

1. The relationship between mass media and society is structured by cultural assumptions about the relationship of the individual to society, about the historical role of the press, about the political economy of the system in question, and about the resultant characteristics of the state.

2. The relationship between the media institution in question and the state, political parties, elites, or other constituencies is an important variable in determining the kind of news that is produced. The "news" will inevitably reflect these constituencies. News may be more or less "objective" based on its relationship to specific constituencies, but no news can be purely objective since subjective individuals organize the news for consumption.

3. Individuals in key positions in mass media organizations also affect media production. They earn their roles because of a fit between themselves and various organizational agendas.

4. The "stories" constructed by the media will reflect the characteristics of the society, institutions, and the individuals comprising them. The evolution of news over time will reflect the amount and direction of social change.

5. The interplay between nations is expressed through mass media institutions; therefore, media can be considered a venue through which leaders "converse"

with one another, and through which reactions to
policies are gauged before their implementation.

Soviet media served as a vehicle for expressing the directives of
leaders such as Brezhnev and Gorbachev. In the process, they reinvented the
Soviet self. Mass media institutions play a critical role in international
relations as channels of communication and dialogue. They have enormous
power to construct political realities and to negotiate them. When tensions
are high between nations, such as was the case between the United States and
the Soviet Union during the Cold War, the mass media may serve as perhaps
the only means of communication available. We can expect the media in the
former Soviet Union (the Commonwealth of Independent States) to
continue to play a central role both in that region and globally.

Bibliography

Alexander, Jeffrey, and Bernhard Giesen. 1987. "From Reduction to Linkage: The Long View of the Micro–Macro Link." In *The Micro–Macro Link* edited by Jeffrey Alexander, et al. Berkeley: University of California Press.

Alexander, Jeffrey, Bernhard Giesen, Richard Munch, and Neil Smelser, eds. 1987. *The Micro–Macro Link*. Berkeley: University of California Press.

Altheide, David L. "Ethnographic Content Analysis." *Qualitative Sociology*, 10 (1), 1987:65–77.

Altheide, David L., and Robert P. Snow. 1979. *Media Logic*. Beverly Hills: Sage Publications.

Althusser, Louis. 1971. *Lenin and Philosophy and Other Essays*. Translated by Ben Brewster. London: New Left Books.

————. 1976. *Essays in Self-Criticism*. Translated by Grahame Lock. London: New Left Books.

Ambler, Effie. 1972. *Russian Journalism and Politics: 1961–1981*. Detroit, Mich.: Wayne State University Press.

Arno, Andrew. 1984. "Communication, Conflict, and Storylines: The News Media as Actors in a Cultural Context." In *The News Media in National and International Conflict* edited by Andrew Arno and Wimal Dissanayake. Boulder, Colo.: Westview Press.

Arno, Andrew, and Wimal Dissanayake, eds. 1984. *The News Media in National and International Conflict*. Boulder, Colo.: Westview Press.

Aubrey, Crispin, ed. 1982. *Nukespeak: The Media and the Bomb*. London: Comedia Publishing Group.

Austin, John. 1962. *How To Do Things with Words*. London: Oxford University Press.

Barron, John. 1974. *K.G.B.: The Secret Work of Soviet Secret Agents*. New York: Reader's Digest Press.

Benford, Robert D., and Lester R. Kurtz. 1984. "Performing the Nuclear Ceremony: The Arms Race as a Ritual." Paper presented at the meetings of the American Sociological Association, San Antonio, Texas.

Berger, Arthur Asa. 1982. *Media Analysis Techniques*. Beverly Hills: Sage Publications.

Berger, Peter, and Thomas Luckman. 1967. *The Social Construction of Reality*. Garden City, N.Y.: Doubleday–Anchor.

Blumer, Herbert. 1969. *Symbolic Interaction: Perspective and Method*. Englewood Cliffs, N.J.: Prentice–Hall.

Bogdanov, N. G. and B. A. Vyazemskii. 1965. *Spravochnik Zhurnalista* (Journalist's Manual), Lenizdat, Leningrad, 166–171.

Bourmeyster, Alexandre. 1988. "Soviet Political Discourse, Narrative Program and the Skaz Theory." In *The Soviet Union: Party and Society* edited by Peter Potichnyj. Cambridge: Cambridge University Press.

Brown, G., and G. Yule. 1983. *Discourse Analysis*. Cambridge: Cambridge University Press.

Cetina, K. Knorr, and Aaron V. Cicourel, eds. 1981. *Advances in Social Theory and Methodology: Toward an Integration of Micro and Macro Sociologies*. Boston: Routledge and Kegan Paul.

Chomsky, Noam. 1965. *Aspects of a Theory of Syntax*. The Hague: Moulton Press.

Cicourel, Aaron V. 1964. *Method and Measurement in Sociology*. New York: The Free Press.

Cohen, Stephen F. 1986. *Sovieticus*. New York: W. W. Norton.

Cohen, Stephen F., and Katrina vanden Heuvel. 1989. *Voices of Glasnost*. New York: W. W. Norton.

Collins, Randall. 1987. "Interaction Ritual Chains, Power and Property: The Micro–Macro Connection as an Empirically Based Theoretical Problem." In *The Micro–Macro Link* edited by Jeffrey Alexander et al. Berkeley: University of California Press.

Conquest, Robert. 1967. *The Politics of Ideas in the U.S.S.R.* New York: Praeger Publishers.

Coser, Lewis. 1984. "Salvation Through Communication?" In *The News Media in National and International Conflict* edited by Andrew Arno and Wimal Dissanayake. Boulder, Colo.: Westview Press.

Coulthard, Malcolm. 1977. *An Introduction to Discourse Analysis*. London: Longman Group Ltd.

Cushman, Thomas O. 1991. "The Orthodox Ethic and the Spirit of Communism." Unpublished research paper.

DeFleur, Melvin and Sandra Ball–Rokeach. 1990. *Theories of Mass Communication*, 4th ed. New York: Longman.

De Sola Pool, Ithiel. 1973. "Communication in Totalitarian Societies." In *Handbook of Communication* edited by I. De Sola Pool, F. Frey, W. Schramm, N. Maccoby, and F. Parker. Chicago: Rand McNally.

Dizard, Wilson P., and S. Blake Swensrud. 1987. *Gorbachev's Information Revolution: Controlling Glasnost in a New Electronic Era*. Boulder,

Colo.: The Center for Strategic and International Studies: Westview Press.

Dodor, Dusko, and Louise Branson. 1990. *Gorbachev: Heretic in the Kremlin*. Harmondsworth, England: Viking Penguin.

Dordick, Herbert. 1984. "New Communications Technology and Media Power." In *The News Media in National and International Conflict* edited by Andrew Arno and Wimal Dissanayake. Boulder, Colo.: Westview Press.

Douglas, Mary. 1986. *How Institutions Think*. Syracuse, N.Y.: Syracuse University Press.

Ebon, Martin. 1987. *The Soviet Propaganda Machine*. New York: McGraw–Hill Book Company.

Feuer, Lewis S. 1964. "Meeting the Philosophers." *Survey* (April 1964). London: Ilford House.

Fitzpatrick, Sheila. 1984. *The Russian Revolution 1917–1932*. Oxford: Oxford University Press.

Foucault, Michel. "Orders of Discourse." *Social Science Information* 10 (1971): 7–30.

———. 1980. *Power/Knowledge: Selected Interviews and Other Writings 1972–1977*. Translated by Colin Gordon. Brighton, England: Harvester.

Friedberg, Maurice, and Hayward Isham, eds. 1987. *Soviet Society Under Gorbachev: Current Trends and Prospects for Reform*. Armonk, N.Y.: M. E. Sharpe.

Gans, Herbert. 1974. *Popular Culture and High Culture*. New York: Basic Books.

———. 1979. *Deciding What's News*. New York: Pantheon Books.

Garfinkel, Harold. 1967. *Studies in Ethnomethodology*. Englewood Cliffs, N.J.: Prentice–Hall.

———. 1974. "On the Origins of the Term 'Ethnomethodology.'" In *Ethnomethodology* edited by Ralph Turner. Harmondsworth, England: Penguin.

Gerbner, George, Ole R. Holsti, Klaus Krippendorff, William J. Paisley, and Philip J. Stone, eds. 1969. *The Analysis of Communication Content*. New York: John Wiley and Sons.

Giddens, Anthony. 1987. "Erving Goffman as a Systematic Social Theorist." In *Social Theory and Modern Sociology*, 109–139. Stanford, Calif.: Stanford University Press.

Giesen, Bernhard. 1987. "Beyond Reductionism: Four Models Relating Micro and Macro Levels." In *The Micro–Macro Link* edited by Jeffrey Alexander, et al. Berkeley: University of California Press.

Gilbert, G. N. and M. Mulkay. 1980. *Opening Pandora's Box: A Sociological Analysis of Scientists' Discourse*. Cambridge: Cambridge University Press.

Gitlin, Todd. 1980. *The Whole World is Watching*. Berkeley: University of California Press.

Goffman, Erving. 1959. *The Presentation of Self in Everyday Life*. New York: Doubleday.

———. 1961. *Asylums*. Harmondsworth, England: Penguin.

———. 1967. *Interaction Ritual*. Garden City, N.Y.: Doubleday.

———. 1971. *Relations in Public: Micro–Studies of the Public Order*. Harmondsworth, England: Penguin.

———. 1974. *Frame Analysis: An Essay on the Organization of Experience*. Cambridge: Harvard University Press.

———. 1981. *Forms of Talk*. Oxford: Blackwell.

Goldfarb, Jeffrey. "Social Bases of Independent Public Expression in Communist Societies." *American Journal of Sociology* 83 (1974):4.

Gorbachev, Mikhail S. 1986. *Political Report of the CPSU Central Committee to the 27th Party Congress*. Moscow: Novosti Press Agency.

———. 1987. *Perestroika: New Thinking for Our Country and the World*. New York: Harper and Row.

Griffith, William. 1973. "Communist Esoteric Communications: Explication de Texte." In *Handbook of Communication* edited by I. De Sola Pool, F. Frey, W. Schramm, N. Maccoby, and F. Parker. Chicago: Rand McNally.

Habermas, Jurgen. 1979. *Communication and the Evolution of Society* edited by Thomas McCarthy. Boston: Beacon.

Hall, Stuart. 1975. "Introduction" to *Paper Voices: The Popular Press and Social Change, 1935–1965* by A. C. H. Smith, E. Immirzi, and T. Blackwell. London: Chatto and Windus.

Hallin, Daniel C., and Paolo Mancini. 1988. "The Summit as Media Event: The Reagan–Gorbachev Meetings on U.S., Italian and Soviet Television." Paper presented at the Second Annual Conference on Nuclear Discourse, Ballyvaughan, Ireland, August 6–12, 1988.

Harris, Richard Jackson. 1989. *A Cognitive Psychology of Mass Communication*. Hillsdale, N.J.: Lawrence Erlbaum Associates, Publishers.

Hart, Roderick P. 1984. *Verbal Style and the Presidency: A Computer Based Analysis*. New York: Academic Press.

Hazan, Baruch A. 1976. *Soviet Propaganda: A Case Study of the Middle East Conflict*. New Brunswick, N.J.: Transaction Books.

———. 1987. *From Brezhnev to Gorbachev: Infighting in the Kremlin*. Boulder, Colo.: Westview Press.

Herman, Edward S. and Frank Brodhead. 1986. *The Rise and Fall of the Bulgarian Connection*. Boston: Sheridan Square Press.

Herman, Edward S., and Noam Chomsky. 1988. *Manufacturing Consent: The Political Economy of the Mass Media*. New York: Pantheon.

Hollander, Gayle D. 1972. *Soviet Political Indoctrination: Developments in Mass Media and Propaganda Since Stalin*. New York: Praeger Publishers.

Hollander, Paul. 1983. *The Many Faces of Socialism: Comparative Sociology and Politics*. New Brunswick, N.J.: Transaction Books.

Hook, Glenn D. 1988. "Roots of Nuclearism: Censorship and Reportage of Atomic Damage in Hiroshima and Nagasaki." La Jolla, Calif.: University of California Institute on Global Conflict and Cooperation.

Hopkins, Mark. 1970. *Mass Media in the Soviet Union*. New York: Western Publishing Company.

Horowitz, Irving Louis. 1964. *The New Sociology: Essays in Social Science and Social Theory in Honor of C. Wright Mills*. New York: Oxford University Press.

Hough, Jerry. "Gorbachev's Strategy." *Foreign Affairs* 64 (1985): 40–55.

Inglis, Fred. 1990. *Media Theory*. Cambridge: Basil Blackwell.

Inkeles, Ales. 1968. *Social Change in Soviet Russia*. Cambridge: Harvard University Press.

Isaacson, Walter. 1989. "A Long, Mighty Struggle." *Time* (April 10, 1989): 49–59.

Johnson, P. 1963. "The Regime and the Intellectuals: A Window on Party Politics." Special Supplement to *Problems of Communism* 4 (1963).

———. *Khruschev and the Arts: The Politics of Soviet Culture, 1962–64*. Cambridge: M. I. T. Press.

Kenez, Peter. 1985. *The Birth of the Propaganda State: Soviet Methods of Mass Mobilization, 1917–1929*. Cambridge: Cambridge University Press.

Koch, Tom. 1990. *The News as Myth*. New York: Greenwood Press.

Korotich, Vitali. 1989. "Typing Out the Fear." *Time* (April 10, 1989): 124.

Kort, Michael. 1990. *The Soviet Colossus: A History of the U.S.S.R.* Boston: Unwin Hyman.

Kurtz, Lester R. 1988. *The Nuclear Cage: A Sociology of the Arms Race*. Englewood Cliffs, N.J.: Prentice–Hall.

Lendvai, Paul. 1981. *The Bureaucracy of Truth: How Communist Countries Manage the News*. London: Burnett Books.

Lenin, Vladimir Ilyich. 1927. *Collected Works*. New York: International Publishers.

———. 1947. *The Essentials of Lenin in Two Volumes*. London: Lawrence & Wishart.

Lewin, Moshe. 1988. *The Gorbachev Phenomenon: A Historical Interpretation.* Berkeley: University of California Press.

Lichtenberg, Judith, ed. 1990. *Democracy and the Mass Media.* Cambridge: Cambridge University Press.

Lincoln, Bruce. 1989. *Discourse and the Construction of Society.* New York: Oxford University Press.

Littrell, W. Boyd, and Gideon Sjoberg, eds. 1976. *Current Issues in Social Policy.* Beverly Hills: Sage.

Littrell, W. Boyd, Gideon Sjoberg, and Louis A. Zurcher, eds. 1983. *Bureaucracy as a Social Problem.* Greenwich, Conn.: JAI Press.

Lotman, Ju M. 1984. "The Role of Dual Models in the Dynamics of Russian Culture." In *The Semiotics of Russian Culture*, edited by A. Shuman. Ann Arbor, Mich.: Slavic Contributions, Number 11.

Luhmann, Niklas. 1987. "The Evolutionary Differentiation between Society." In *The Micro–Macro Link* edited by Jeffrey Alexander et al. Berkeley: University of California Press.

Macdonnell, Diane. 1986. *Theories of Discourse.* Oxford: Basil Blackwell Ltd.

Manoff, Robert Karl. 1988. "Reporting the Other by Denying the Self." *Deadline* 3 (Jan.–Feb. 1988):1.

Marinov, Vsevolod. 1989. "What the Comrades Say." *Time* (April 10, 1989): 62–63.

Markham, James W. 1967. *Voices of the Red Giants: Communications in Russia and China.* Ames, Iowa: Iowa State University Press.

Matthews, Mervyn. 1978. *Privilege in the Soviet Union: A Study of Elite Life Styles Under Communism.* London: George Allen and Unwin.

Mead, George Herbert. 1934. *Mind, Self, and Society from the Standpoint of a Social Behaviorist.* Edited and with an introduction by Charles W. Morris. Chicago: University of Chicago Press.

———. 1936. *Movements of Thought in the Nineteenth Century.* Edited and with an introduction by Merritt H. Moore. Chicago: University of Chicago Press.

Mehan, Hugh, and James M. Skelly. 1988. "Reykjavik: The Breach and Repair of the Pure War Script." La Jolla, Calif.: Institute on Global Conflict and Cooperation.

Mehan, Hugh, and Houston Wood. 1975. *The Reality of Ethnomethodology.* New York: Wiley.

Mickiewicz, Ellen P. 1988. *Split Signals: Television and Politics in the Soviet Union.* Oxford: Oxford University Press.

———. 1973. *Handbook of Soviet Social Science Data.* New York: The Free Press.

———. 1981. *Media and the Russian Public.* New York: Praeger.

———. 1987. "Making the Media Work: Soviet Society and Communications." In *Soviet Society Under Gorbachev: Current*

Trends and Prospects For Reform, edited by M. Friedberg and H. Isham. Armonk, N.Y.: M.E. Sharpe.

Mickiewicz, Ellen P., and Gregory Haley. "Soviet and American News: Week of Intensive Interaction." *Slavic Review* 46 no. 2 (1987):214–228.

Mills, C. Wright. 1956. *The Power Elite*. New York: Oxford University Press.

———. 1957. "Situated Actions and Vocabularies of Motive." In *Power, Politics and People: The Collected Essays of C. Wright Mills* edited by Irving Louis Horowitz. New York: Oxford University Press.

———. 1959. *The Sociological Imagination*. New York: Oxford University Press.

———. 1962. *The Marxists*. New York: Dell Publishing Co.

Moscow News, 1972–1974; 1988–1991. Moscow: Union of Societies for Friendship and Cultural Relations with Foreign Countries and Novosti Press Agency.

Mowlana, Hamid. 1984. "Communication, World Order, and the Human Potential: Toward an Ethical Framework." In *The News Media in National and International Conflict* edited by Andrew Arno and Wimal Dissanayake. Boulder: Westview Press.

Nathanson, Charles E. 1988. "The Social Construction of the 'Soviet Threat': A Study in the Politics of Representation." La Jolla, Calif.: University of California Institute on Global Conflict and Cooperation.

"Novosti Press Agency Statute." 1980. Moscow: Novosti Press Agency.

Oberg, James E. 1988. *Uncovering Soviet Disasters: Exploring the Limits of Glasnost*. New York: Random House.

Olcott, Anthony. 1987. "Glasnost and Soviet Culture." In *Soviet Society Under Gorbachev: Current Trends and Prospects for Reform* edited by M. Friedberg and H. Isham, 101–103. Armonk, N.Y.: M. E. Sharpe.

Pankhurst, Jerry G., and Michael P. Sacks. 1980. *Contemporary Soviet Society: Sociological Perspectives*. New York: Praeger Publishers.

Parenti, Michael. 1986. *Inventing Reality: The Politics of the Mass Media*. New York: St. Martin's Press.

Pecheux, M. 1982. *Language, Semantics, and Ideology: Stating the Obvious*. London: Macmillan Press.

Plummer, Ken. 1983. *Documents of Life: An Introduction to the Problems and Literature of a Humanistic Method*. London: George Allen & Unwin.

Potichnyj, Peter, ed. 1988. *The Soviet Union Party and Society*. Cambridge: Cambridge University Press.

Potter, Jonathon, and Margaret Wetherell. 1987. *Discourse and Social Psychology*. London: Sage Publications.

Remington, Thomas. 1986. "Soviet Public Opinion and the Effectiveness of Party Ideological Work." University of Pittsburgh: The Carl Beck Papers in Russian and East European Studies, Number 204.

———. 1988. *The Truth of Authority: Ideology and Communication in the Soviet Union*. Pittsburgh: University of Pittsburgh Press.

Remnick, David. 1991. "The Gorbachev Flock: Their God is Dead." *International Herald Tribune* (April 3, 1991): 1.

Richardson, Kay. 1988. "The Mikhail and Maggie Show: The British Popular Press and the Anglo–Soviet Summit." La Jolla, Calif.: University of California Institute on Global Conflict and Cooperation.

Roxburgh, Angus. 1987. *Pravda: Inside the Soviet News Machine*. London: Victor Gollancz Ltd.

Saussure, Ferdinand de. 1974. *Course in General Linguistics*, Translated by Wade Baskin (1916). London: Fontana.

Schudson, Michael. 1978. *Discovering the News: A Social History of American Newspapers*. New York: Basic Books.

Schutz. Alfred. 1962. *Collected Papers, Volume I: The Problem of Social Reality*. The Hague: M. Nijhoff.

Shanor, Donald R. 1985. *Behind the Lines: The Private War against Soviet Censorship*. New York: St. Martin's Press.

Shapiro. Michael J. 1988. *The Politics of Representation*. Madison, Wisc.: University of Wisconsin Press.

Shlapentokh, Vladimir. 1987. *The Politics of Sociology in the Soviet Union*. Boulder, Colo.: Westview Press.

Simirenko, Alex, ed. 1966. *Soviet Sociology: Historical Antecedents and Current Appraisals*. Chicago: Quadrangle Books.

Simmel, Georg. 1950. *Sociology*. Glencoe: The Free Press.

———. 1968. *Conflict in Modern Culture and Other Essays*. Translated and with an introduction by Peter Etzkorn. New York: Teachers College Press.

———. 1980. *Essays on Interpretation in Social Science*. Translated and with an Introduction by Guy Oakes. Totowa, N.J.: Rowman and Littlefield.

Sipchen, Bob. "An As-is View of Soviet Life." *Los Angeles Times* (26 April 1990: E 6).

Sivachev, Nikolai V., and Nikolai N. Yakovlev. 1979. *Russia and the United States: U.S.–Soviet Relations from the Soviet Point of View*. Chicago: University of Chicago Press.

Sjoberg, Gideon, ed. 1967. *Ethics, Politics, and Social Research*. Cambridge: Schenkman Publishing Co.

Sjoberg, Gideon, and Roger Nett. 1968. *A Methodology for Social Research*. New York: Harper and Row.

Sjoberg, Gideon, Ted R. Vaughan, and Norma Williams. "Bureaucracy as a Moral Issue." *The Journal of Applied Behavioral Science* 20, no. 4 (1984):441–453.

Skelly, James M. 1989. "Hungarian Television News: Its Role in the Current Transformation and the Implications for Domestic and International Affairs." Unpublished research proposal.

Skilling, H. Gordon. 1989. *Samizdat and an Independent Society in Central and Eastern Europe*. London: Macmillan Press.

Sorokin, Pitirim. 1966. "Russian Sociology in the Twentieth Century." In *Soviet Sociology* edited by Alex Simirenko, 45–55. Chicago: Quadrangle Books.

Sovetskaya Pechat, vol. 3 (1961):50.

Soviet Life, 1972–1974; 1988–1991. Moscow: Novosti Press Agency.

Strong, Tracy, and Helene Keyssar. 1983. *Right in Her Soul: The Life of Anna Louise Strong*. New York: Random House.

Stubbs, M. 1983. *Discourse Analysis*. Oxford: Blackwell.

Tannen, D. 1984. *Coherence in Spoken and Written Discourse*. Norwood, N.J.: Ablex.

Tarasulo, Isaac J., ed. 1989. *Gorbachev and Glasnost: Viewpoints from the Soviet Press*. Wilmington: Scholarly Resource Books.

Tehranian, Majid. 1984. "Events, Pseudo–events, Media Events: Image Politics and the Future of International Diplomacy." In *The News Media in National and International Conflict* edited by Andrew Arno and Wimal Dissanayake. Boulder, Colo.: Westview Press.

Tuchman, Gaye. 1978. *Making News: A Study in the Construction of Reality*. New York: The Free Press.

Tucker, Robert C., ed. 1978. *The Marx–Engels Reader*. New York: W. W. Norton.

Turpin, Jennifer. 1994. "Glasnost and the End of the Cold War." In *Rethinking Peace* edited by Robert Elias and Jennifer Turpin. Boulder, Colo: Lynne Rienner Publishers.

———. 1990. "Gorbachev and the Soviet Media Revolution." *Peace Review*, (August 1990): 15–18.

Urban, Michael E. 1988. "Political Language and Political Change in the USSR: Notes on the Gorbachev Leadership." In *The Soviet Union: Party and Society* edited by Peter Potichnyj. Cambridge: Cambridge University Press.

van Dijk, Teun A., ed. 1977. *Text and Context Explorations in the Semantics and Pragmatics of Discourse*. London: Longman Group Ltd.

———. 1980. *Macrostructures*. Hillsdale, N.J.: Lawrence Erlbaum Associates Publishers.

———. 1985a. *Handbook of Discourse Analysis Volumes 1–4*. London: Academic Press.

———.1985b. *Discourse and Communication*. Berlin: Walter de Gruyter.

———. 1988. *News as Discourse*. Hillsdale, N.J.: L. Erlbaum Associates.

Vaughan, Ted R., and Gideon Sjoberg. 1984. "The Individual and Bureaucracy: An Alternative Meadian Interpretation." *The Journal of Applied Behavioral Science* 10, no. 1 (1984):57–69.

Veblen, Thorstein. 1955. "The Theory of the Leisure Class." In *Man in Contemporary Society: A Source Book*, 699–725. New York: Columbia University Press.

Volosinov, Valentin Nikolaevich. 1930. *Marxism and the Philosophy of Language,* Translated by Ladislav Matejka and I. R. Titunik (1973). New York: Seminar Press.

Weber, Max. 1946. "Bureaucracy." In *From Max Weber: Essays in Sociology*, translated and edited by H. H. Gerth and C. Wright Mills. New York: Oxford University Press, 196–244.

———. 1977. *Basic Concepts in Sociology*. Translated by H. P. Secher. Westport, Conn.: Greenwood Press.

Wheatcroft, S. G. 1983. "Towards a Thorough Analysis of Soviet Forced Labour Statistics." *Soviet Studies* 35 no. 2 (1983): 223–237.

White, Stephen. 1988. "Political Socialization in the USSR: April 1979 and After." In *The Soviet Union: Party and Society* edited by Peter Potichnyj. Cambridge: Cambridge University Press.

Williams, Norma, Gideon Sjoberg, and Andre Sjoberg. 1983. "The Bureaucratic Personality." In *Bureaucracy as a Social Problem* edited by W. Boyd Littrell, Gideon Sjoberg, and Louis A. Zurcher. Greenwich, Conn.: JAI Press, 173–189.

Zaslavsky, Victor. 1982. "Closed Cities and the Organized Consensus." In *The Neo–Stalinist State* edited by V. Zaslavsky. Armonk, N.J.: M. E. Sharpe, Inc.

Zhurnalist, vol. 1 (1972):5.

Zimmermann, Rudiger. 1988. "Selling 'SDI' to Europeans: Arguments, Metaphors and Adversary Images." La Jolla, Calif.: Institute on Global Conflict and Cooperation.

Zinoviev, Alexander. 1984. *The Reality of Communism*. New York: Schocken Books.

———. 1985. *Homo Sovieticus*. Translated and with an introduction by Charles Janson. Boston: Atlantic Monthly Press.

Index

About the Author

JENNIFER TURPIN is Assistant Professor of Sociology and coordinator of the Women's Studies Program at the University of San Francisco. She has been active in teaching, researching, and writing about peace, Russian society, media, and social change.

ISBN 0-275-95043-3

9 780275 950439

HARDCOVER BAR CODE